F. A. Hayek

Series Introduction

The *Major Conservative and Libertarian Thinkers* series aims to show that there is a rigorous, scholarly tradition of social and political thought that may be broadly described as "conservative", "libertarian" or some combination of the two.

The series aims to show that conservatism is not simply a reaction against contemporary events, nor a privileging of intuitive thought over deductive reasoning; libertarianism is not simply an apology for unfettered capitalism or an attempt to justify a misguided atomistic concept of the individual. Rather, the thinkers in this series have developed coherent intellectual positions that are grounded in empirical reality and also founded upon serious philosophical reflection on the relationship between the individual and society, how the social institutions necessary for a free society are to be established and maintained, and the implications of the limits to human knowledge and certainty.

Each volume in the series presents a thinker's ideas in an accessible and cogent manner to provide an indispensable work for students with varying degrees of familiarity with the topic as well as more advanced scholars.

The following twenty volumes that make up the entire *Major Conservative and Libertarian Thinkers* series are written by international scholars and experts:

The Salamanca School by Andre Azevedo Alves (LSE, UK) and
   José Manuel Moreira (Universidade de Aveiro, Portugal)
Thomas Hobbes by R. E. R. Bunce (Cambridge, UK)
John Locke by Eric Mack (Tulane, UK)
David Hume by Christopher J. Berry (Glasgow, UK)
Adam Smith by James Otteson (Yeshiva, US)
Edmund Burke by Dennis O'Keeffe (Buckingham, UK)
Alexis de Tocqueville by Alan S Kahan (Paris, France)
Herbert Spencer by Alberto Mingardi (Istituto Bruno Leoni, Italy)

Ludwig von Mises by Richard Ebeling (Northwood, US)
Joseph A. Schumpeter by John Medearis (Riverside, California, US)
F. A. Hayek by Adam Tebble (UCL, UK)
Michael Oakeshott by Edmund Neill (Oxford, UK)
Karl Popper by Phil Parvin (Loughborough, UK)
Ayn Rand by Mimi Gladstein (Texas, US)
Milton Friedman by William Ruger (Texas State, US)
Russell Kirk by John Pafford (Northwood, US)
James M. Buchanan by John Meadowcroft (King's College London, UK)
The Modern Papacy by Samuel Gregg (Acton Institute, US)
Murray Rothbard by Gerard Casey (UCD, Ireland)
Robert Nozick by Ralf Bader (St Andrews, UK)

Of course, in any series of this nature, choices have to be made as to which thinkers to include and which to leave out. Two of the thinkers in the series – F. A. Hayek and James M. Buchanan – have written explicit statements rejecting the label "conservative". Similarly, other thinkers, such as David Hume and Karl Popper, may be more accurately described as classical liberals than either conservatives or libertarians. But these thinkers have been included because a full appreciation of this particular tradition of thought would be impossible without their inclusion; conservative and libertarian thought cannot be fully understood without some knowledge of the intellectual contributions of Hume, Hayek, Popper and Buchanan, among others. While no list of conservative and libertarian thinkers can be perfect, then, it is hoped that the volumes in this series come as close as possible to providing a comprehensive account of the key contributors to this particular tradition.

John Meadowcroft
King's College London

F. A. Hayek

A. J. Tebble

Major Conservative and
Libertarian Thinkers
Series Editor: John Meadowcroft
Volume 13

continuum

2010

The Continuum International Publishing Group Inc
80 Maiden Lane, New York, NY 10038

The Continuum International Publishing Group Ltd
The Tower Building, 11 York Road, London SE1 7NX

www.continuumbooks.com

ISBN: 978-1-4411-0906-4

Library of Congress Cataloging-in-Publication Data
Tebble, A. J.
F. A. Hayek / A. J. Tebble.
p. cm. – (Major conservative and libertarian thinkers ; v. 13)
Includes bibliographical references and index.
ISBN-13: 978-0-8264-3599-6 (hardcover : alk. paper)
ISBN-10: 0-8264-3599-8 (hardcover : alk. paper)
1. Hayek, Friedrich A. von (Friedrich August),
1899–1992—Political and social views.
I. Title. II. Series.
JC273.H382T44 2010
320.51′2092—dc22   2009053798

Typeset by Newgen Imaging Systems Pvt Ltd, Chennai, India

For My Parents

Contents

Series Editor's Preface

F. A. Hayek was one of the most significant thinkers of the twentieth century. In a phenomenally productive working life that spanned seven decades, Hayek made important contributions to economics, politics, philosophy, law, the history of ideas, the philosophy of science and evolutionary psychology. Among Hayek's most enduring contributions were his account of the epistemological role of market prices in enabling people to overcome the coordination problems inherent to an advanced economy with a profound division of labour; his description of the processes that led free societies to become totalitarian regimes; his critique of the notion of social justice as a legitimate goal of public policy; and his explanation of the way in which complex social systems evolve as spontaneous orders rather than through conscious direction.

Although Hayek's intellectual achievements cannot be doubted, he may seem a strange choice for inclusion in this series given that in a postscript to one of his most famous works, *The Constitution of Liberty*, Hayek explicitly rejected conservatism. Hayek was not a conservative because conservatism provided no account of an ideal society or a set of social institutions that could be used as a standard against which to judge others. Rather, conservatives sought only to preserve the institutions that happened to exist in a particular society at a particular time. Whereas at heart conservatism is a culturally relativist philosophy, then, Hayek believed in the universality of classical liberal principles and institutions. Hayek recognized that in a contemporary context this very often gave him common cause with European and North American conservatives who also wished to preserve those institutions, but he was aware that he would have little in common with conservatives in a society where those institutions had not been established.

Hayek's thought, then, can be said to make an important contribution to the Western conservative tradition in that he opposed the decline of classical liberal values and institutions in those societies in the twentieth century, but Hayek was not a philosophical conservative.

Rather, Hayek may be more accurately described as a classical liberal or (to use his own preferred term) a Whig, or in contemporary parlance he fits quite comfortably in the libertarian tradition. Hayek did believe in universal principles of just government and for Hayek those universal principles were the Whig values of the rule of law, constitutionally limited government and *laissez-faire*.

Providing a thorough account of the thought of a thinker as sophisticated, prolific and wide-ranging as Hayek is not an easy task, but in this outstanding account of Hayek's life and work, Adam James Tebble of the University of Buckingham has risen to the challenge brilliantly. Tebble sets out the central features of Hayek's intellectual contributions in the context of Hayek's life and times. In so doing, he vividly captures the subtleties and nuances of one of the most original and insightful thinkers of the twentieth century.

This volume makes a crucial contribution to the Major Conservative and Libertarian Thinkers series by setting out the thought of one of the most innovative contributors to this tradition. In presenting Hayek's ideas in such an accessible and cogent form, Tebble has produced an outstanding volume that will prove indispensable to those relatively unfamiliar with Hayek's work as well as more advanced scholars.

John Meadowcroft
King's College London

Acknowledgements

Writing this book would not have been possible without the extraordinarily generous support of the Thomas W. Smith Foundation of New York, who awarded me a Hayek Scholarship in the 2007/2008 year to begin work on this project. Special thanks are also due to Richard Bellamy at UCL's School of Public Policy for providing me with such a productive working environment over the last two years, and to C. Bradley Thompson, Director of Clemson University's Clemson Institute for the Study of Capitalism, for his support and encouragement during my stay there as a Visiting Scholar in the Spring Semester of the 2008/2009 year. Gratitude is owed also to the Institute for Humane Studies and to James Piereson, for their support during the course of this project.

Special debts are owed to Mark Pennington and Phil Parvin for reading previous versions of a number of the chapters of this book, and to everyone with whom I have discussed Hayek's ideas, and from whom I have learned so much. Special mention in this regard must be made of Pete Boettke, Jason Brennan, Corey Brettschneider, John Charvet, Philip Cook, Paolo Dardanelli, Jurgen De Wispelaere, David Estlund, Andrew Gamble, John Gray, Paul Kelly, Sharon Krause, Hans Kribbe, Chandran Kukathas, Eric Mack, Carmen Pavel, Keith Shaw, John Tomasi, Nikolai Wenzel and Mariah Zeisberg. Lastly, I would like to thank series editor John Meadowcroft and Marie-Claire Antoine of Continuum Press for all their invaluable feedback and support.

A. J. Tebble

1

Hayek's Life and Times

Introduction

Even by the standards of his day Friedrich Hayek's thought was wide-ranging and covered fields as diverse as economics, psychology, jurisprudence and social and political theory. Yet, despite this heterogeneity, underlying his intellectual contribution is a unifying philosophical approach centred upon a conception of mind and of the nature of reason. It is to this foundational aspect of Heyek's thought, then, that attention must be paid if one is to understand his wider contributions. Regrettably, in an introductory text, there is only so much in-depth critical appraisal that one can undertake. For this reason, and by setting out his views on a variety of topics and appraising them where possible, the main purpose of this book will be to familiarise the reader with the principal themes of Hayek's thought and to ascertain the extent to which his contributions may be considered to form a coherent system.

Family Background and Early Education 1899–1918

Hayek was born the eldest of three brothers in Vienna, Austria-Hungary, on 8 May 1899 into a nominally Roman Catholic family that had been ennobled towards the end of the eighteenth century. His family also contained a number of prominent intellectuals working in the fields of statics and, in particular, biology. Heyek's paternal grandfather, Gustav von Hayek, studied natural history and biology and taught at a *Gymnasium* (Secondary School). He was also the pioneer of ornithology in Austria, having been secretary general at the first International Ornithology Congress in Vienna in 1884. Hayek's father, Dr August Hayek, was a physician and botanist who also published a major botanical treatise while working as a doctor in the government's social welfare system. He later secured an unpaid honorary professorship, or *Privatdozent*, in botany at the University of Vienna, although he never achieved a hoped-for chair. Hayek's maternal grandfather, Franz von Juraschek was a professor of public law at the University of Innsbruck and, later, the first head of Austria–Hungary's National Statistical Office. Given the social expectations of the day, Hayek's mother, Felicitas Juraschek, was like most women not involved professionally in academia. Nevertheless, it was she who was primarily responsible for cultivating the intellectual environment in the home. Through her, Hayek was also second cousin to the philosopher Ludwig Wittgenstein, with whom he remained in sporadic contact until just after the end of World War II.

Given this intensely intellectual background it is no surprise that both of Hayek's younger brothers also became professors; Heinz teaching anatomy at the University of Vienna, Erich teaching chemistry at the University of Innsbruck. Hayek himself, however, was not the best of students, gaining a reputation for laziness and ill-discipline, despite demonstrating clear ability. Like many able but essentially uninterested students Hayek also embarked upon studies of his own in a wide variety of fields including drama, botany and palaeontology. This was to be an intellectual trait that would remain with him for the rest of his life. Significantly, it was also early on that Hayek had become acquainted with economics, evolutionary theory and psychology, having briefly studied them in 1916. These would all be subjects that would later have a profound and lasting impact.

Before completing his secondary education, Hayek lied about his age and joined a field artillery unit in the Austro-Hungarian army in March 1917, almost three years after the start of World War I. After seven months of training he spent a little over a year on the Italian front, almost all of it on the left bank of the Piave River. Despite some dangerous encounters Hayek survived the Great War without serious injury and even managed whilst on leave in the autumn of 1917 to return to his *Gymnasium* in order to receive the certification that would permit him to attend university the following year. His brief stay at the *Gymnasium*, however, did not pass without incident, with Hayek being reprimanded for reading a socialist pamphlet during a divinity class. More seriously, in the summer of 1918 following a failed Austrian offensive against Italy, Hayek came down with influenza, being just one of the many millions who did so during the great worldwide pandemic that occurred at this time. To compound matters he also contracted malaria during the October retreat subsequent to the Battle of the Piave River, the most decisive battle of World War I on the Italian front. Hayek earned a decoration for bravery and it was his experience coordinating communications for his unit in the multilingual Austro-Hungarian army that turned his interest to social science and political ideas. 'I served in a battle in which eleven different languages were spoken' and which was 'bound to draw your attention to the problems of political organisation', he was to comment years later.[1]

University Education and Early Career 1918–1931

After being discharged from the army in October 1918, Hayek decided to pursue an academic career and entered the Arts Faculty of the University of Vienna a month later. Initially wanting to become a diplomat, Hayek's first choice of study was cut-off by the disappearance of the *Konsularakademis* (Diplomatic School) in the wake of the post-war collapse of Austria–Hungary. He was thus left with the choice of either psychology or economics but again found his hand forced by circumstance. Because there was no-one left at the university to teach psychology after the war, Hayek opted for law, as this at least included the study of economics.

The Winter of 1919–1920 was a particularly hard one and, to escape Vienna's shortages of food and fuel (which forced the closure of the university), as well as to help him recuperate from the lingering effects of malaria, Hayek's family arranged for the 20 year-old to travel to Zurich. Here Hayek attended lectures on law and philosophy and also worked in the laboratory of the brain anatomist Constantin Monakow, tracing fibre bundles in the different parts of the human brain. The draft research paper that resulted – 'Contribution towards a theory of how consciousness develops' – was set aside that September so that Hayek could prepare for some law exams.[2] Despite lying dormant for a quarter of a century, this paper would become the basis for subsequent work in theoretical psychology that Hayek recommenced in 1946 and which would eventually be published as *The Sensory Order* in 1952. Hayek also travelled to Norway where in the late summer of 1920 he finally shook off his malaria and acquired sufficient knowledge of Scandinavian languages to translate a book on inflation by Swedish economist and pioneer of the idea of purchasing power parity, Gustav Cassel.

It was in 1921 whilst completing his first degree in Law in three rather than the customary four years that Hayek decided to look for work. He was aided in this venture by one of his professors, Friedrich Wieser, who provided him with a letter of introduction to the leading figure of what had come to be called the Austrian School of economics, Ludwig Mises. At that time Mises was working as a representative of the Chamber of Commerce in the *Abrechnungsamt* (Office of Accounts) whose purpose was to implement the financial provisions of the Treaty of St Germain which oversaw the break-up of the Austro-Hungarian Empire after the Great War. Wieser's letter described Hayek as a promising young economist, and Hayek never tired of recounting Mises's response: 'Wieser says you're a promising young economist. I've never seen you at my lectures.'[3] In fact, Hayek *had* attended some of Mises' lectures, but given his leftist political sympathies, regarded the economist's liberal views as somewhat extreme. This was soon to change, however, with the publication in 1922 of Mises' book *Socialism*, where he argued that without the price mechanism of the market, economic calculation under socialism would face insurmountable difficulties. Hayek was later to say that this book 'gradually but fundamentally altered the outlook of many of the young idealists returning to their university studies after World War I. I know, for I was one of them.'[4] 'We felt,' he was to write in the Foreword to a subsequent edition of *Socialism*,

> that the civilization in which we had grown up had collapsed. We were determined to build a better world, and it was this desire to reconstruct society that led many of us to the study of economics. Socialism promised to fulfil our hopes for a more rational, more just world. And then came this book. Our hopes had been dashed. *Socialism* told us that we had been looking for improvement in the wrong direction.[5]

During this 18-month period between 1921 and 1923 in which he worked for Mises, Hayek also wrote his doctoral dissertation in political science, thus receiving his second degree in the spring of 1923. It was also in 1921 that Hayek helped to set up an informal meeting group called the *Geistkreis*, or 'Mind Circle', many of whose participants were later to leave Austria for the United States in the lead up to World War II, and become highly respected in their fields. These included Fritz Machlup and other young students such as Gottfried Haberler, Erich

Vogelin, Alfred Schutz, Oskar Morgenstern and Felix Kaufmann.[6] By the time he had received his doctorate Hayek had decided to be an economist and to improve his knowledge of the subject, as well as his English, also decided to visit the United States. Hayek set off in March 1923 for New York, where he stayed for the following 14 months and worked as a research assistant to Professor Jeremiah Jenks, of New York University, to whom Hayek had been introduced by Mises when Jenks passed through Vienna in the spring of 1922. After working with Jenks, Hayek enrolled as a scholarship student at New York University and also attended lectures at Columbia University and the New School of Social Research. Despite having to live on a limited budget, Hayek had hoped to extend his stay by securing a Rockefeller Fellowship. In fact, he was the first proposed candidate from Austria for a fellowship but news of his success came only after he had commenced his return to Vienna. Significantly, it was during his time in the United States that Hayek came to be deeply interested in the causes of economic fluctuations, or 'business cycles', and the kinds of policy needed to address them, particularly as these related to monetary theory. Returning to Vienna in the summer of 1924, Hayek resumed his post at the *Abrechnungsamt* and, importantly, gained admittance to Mises' *Privatseminar* along with many of his *Geistkreis* friends. This seminar, which took place at Mises' offices in the Chamber of Commerce and was held on a fortnightly basis until 1931 had started at about the time *Socialism* was published. Attendance at the seminar was to further consolidate the influence Mises had upon Hayek.

In 1926 Hayek married his first wife, Helene Fritsch, with whom he would have two children. Having helped Mises to establish it, Hayek then became the first director of the Austrian Institute for Business Cycle Research in January 1927. In 1928 Hayek was invited to a conference on economic statistics in London, where he met economist John Maynard Keynes for the first time, as well as the director of the LSE and future architect of the British welfare state, William Beveridge. In 1929 the 30-year-old Hayek was admitted to the University of Vienna as a *Privatdozent* in economics and statistics. To qualify for this post he gave a public lecture on 'The Paradox of Saving' which critiqued the then prevalent view that economic downturns occurred because people saved too much and spent too little. These themes were given a more comprehensive treatment in Hayek's first book on the trade cycle, *Monetary Theory and the Trade Cycle*, which was originally published in German as *Geldtheorie und Konjunkturtheorie*. Significantly, Hayek was one of the few economists who, as early as February 1929, gave warning of the possibility of a major economic crisis before the onset of the Great Depression the following autumn.[7]

The LSE and Cambridge 1931–1950

In a coincidence that would change the course of his life and career, a published version of Hayek's lecture on the paradox of saving caught the attention of another gifted scholar, Lionel Robbins, who at the time was the youngest professor of economics in England. Perhaps most significantly for the future course of Hayek's career, Robbins had become Chair of the Department of Economics at the London School of Economics in 1929. Robbins and Hayek were not only close in age, but also in intellectual sympathies. Like Hayek, Robbins had been influenced by Mises' *Socialism* and was sympathetic to the Austrian School in general. Because of this and his eagerness to counter-balance the influence of Keynes and his followers in Cambridge, Robbins invited Hayek to give a series of guest lectures at the LSE in February 1931. Hayek surveyed the history of monetary theory and introduced English-speaking economists to the Austrian view that economic fluctuations were largely driven by monetary fluctuations, and that depression was the inevitable consequence of prior inflation. Before this, however, Hayek first went to Cambridge in 1930 where he gave some lectures that were explicitly critical of Keynes's analysis of the Great Depression. Unsurprisingly, Hayek's views were not well-received in the heartland of Keynesian economics and marked the first of several encounters between two rival schools of thought.

According to Robbins Hayek's LSE lectures caused a sensation both for their difficulty and their novelty. With Robbins' encouragement the lectures were published as Hayek's first book in English, *Prices and Production* (1931, 1935), and included a Foreword by Robbins himself. Following these early successes, Hayek was offered the post of visiting professor at the LSE for the 1931–1932 year, thus becoming the first foreign faculty member in the economics department. Beveridge then suggested to Robbins the idea of inviting Hayek to stay on at the LSE as a permanent member of the faculty. The vote in his favour was unanimous, and Heyek became the Tooke Professor of Economic Science and Statistics in 1932. Whilst at the LSE, Hayek and Robbins organized a weekly seminar similar to Mises'. The seminar was not only intended for British economists but also for those from abroad, and through this Hayek kept up his acquaintance with old colleagues from Vienna such as Haberler and Machlup. Economist John Kenneth Galbraith also attended the seminar in 1937 and 1938, describing it as possibly the most verbally aggressive encounter in the entire history of the teaching of economics.[8] In 1936 Hayek also invited the philosopher and fellow-Austrian Karl Popper to speak at another seminar that he ran alone. Popper there presented an early version of what would later become his book *The Poverty of Historicism*. It was also Hayek who, along with art Historian and fellow Viennese, Ernst Gombrich, helped Popper find a publisher for this work and persuaded colleagues at the London School of Economics to give him a teaching position.[9]

Throughout the 1930s, Hayek devoted most of his energies to exploring the theories of money and capital. His 1929 book on the trade cycle appeared in English as *Monetary Theory and the Trade Cycle* (1933). Following this Hayek delivered five lectures at the *Institut Universitaire de Hautes Études Internationales* in Geneva, where Mises had gone in 1934 after Hitler had come to power in Germany. The Geneva lectures were eventually published as *Monetary Nationalism and International Stability* (1937). Hayek's *Profits, Interest and Investment and Other Essays on the Theory of Industrial Fluctuations* came out in 1939 and *The Pure Theory of Capital* in 1941. Also notable was the 1935 publication of his edited volume *Collectivist Economic Planning: Critical Studies on the Possibilities of Socialism*. This book criticized central planning for its inability to make use of the knowledge necessary for rational economic calculation and would become one of the central texts in what came to be known as the Socialist Calculation Debate. It was no surprise, then, that the 1930s saw Hayek earn a considerable reputation, becoming, along with Keynes, one of the world's leading economists. Nevertheless, his contributions, and particularly his critical reviews of Keynes' *A Treatise on Money*, were not received well by the latter's followers in Cambridge and, for reasons that will be explored elsewhere in this book, by the end of the decade Hayek's reputation had begun to diminish. Crucially, this change was accompanied by an ever-diminishing interest on his part in the more formal aspects of the discipline and emphasis instead on the philosophical underpinnings of economic enquiry. This change was particularly apparent in one of his most enduringly significant papers, 'Economics and Knowledge' (1936). This paper, Hayek was to remark later, heralded an entirely new theoretical departure for him, insofar as it launched a profound critique of the neo-classical concept of general equilibrium that underpinned much of the dominant economic theory and practice of the day.

Unwilling to return to Austria after its annexation by, and subsequent *Anschluss* with, Nazi Germany in 1938, Hayek became a British citizen that same year, a status he was to hold for the remainder of his life. With the onset of World War II, the LSE was transferred to Peterhouse College, Cambridge and Hayek initially commuted there from London three days a week. However, with the bombing of the British capital in 1940, he moved to Cambridge permanently, spending the rest of the war there. For the first year, the Hayeks had to rely on the Robbins' generosity in providing them with accommodation in their cottage in the Chilterns. Given the clear intellectual differences between the LSE and Cambridge at this time, transferring there may have been a little daunting. Yet, despite this Keynes and Hayek enjoyed a good personal relationship and it was Keynes who, as administrator of King's College, secured accommodation for the Hayeks.

It was during this period that one of Hayek's best known works, *The Road to Serfdom*, originated. Hayek was concerned about the general view in Britain that national-socialism was a capitalist reaction against socialism, and that central planning presented no danger to liberal democracy; and had outlined his views in an earlier paper entitled 'Freedom and the Economic System' (1939). *The Road to Serfdom* was written between 1940 and 1943 and the title came from the French thinker Alexis de Tocqueville's writings in the previous century on the 'road to servitude' in *Democracy in America*. It was first published in Britain by Routledge in March 1944 and was quite popular, leading Hayek to call it 'that unobtainable book', although this was also due to wartime paper rationing. When it was published in the United States in September 1944, *The Road to Serfdom* was far more popular than it had been in Britain, though it received far more critical reviews, including an infamous one entitled *The Road to Reaction* by Hayek's LSE colleague Herman Finer.[10]

The year 1944 was also significant for Hayek because it marked the start of a process that would culminate in the founding of a movement to promote liberal ideas worldwide and it was at a meeting of King's College Political Society where Hayek first broached the idea.

Over the next three years the idea for this society would undergo various permutations until, in April 1947, Hayek organized a meeting of scholars concerned with individual liberty. Part of the impetus for this were his encounters with many people, in both Europe and the United States, whom he had met consequent to the notoriety Hayek had gained for *The Road to Serfdom* and who shared his views but felt isolated politically. Thirty-nine participants from 10 countries gathered at the Hôtel du Parc, Mont-Pèlerin sur Vevey, near Montreux, Switzerland for the first meeting. Among them were Robbins, Popper, Mises, scientist and philosopher Michael Polanyi, Milton Friedman, *Newsweek* columnist Henry Hazlitt and economists Frank H. Knight and George J. Stigler. There was considerable debate about how much government intervention in the economy would be compatible with a free society, with the Americans being more radical than the Europeans. Despite such disagreements on specific policies, it was agreed to form a group who would continue to meet and whose name, in a compromise, would be the Mont Pèlerin Society. Four of the original members – Hayek, Friedman, Stigler and Maurice Allais – later won Nobel Prizes, and over the years Mont Pèlerin Society members did much to lead the revival of interest in classical liberalism.

Chicago 1950–1962

By the late 1940s, Hayek had begun to grow stale as an economist and, in keeping with his multidisciplinary background and training, ventured into other fields of enquiry. In 1950 after divorcing his wife and remarrying, Hayek left the London School of Economics for the United States, initially spending a semester at the University of Arkansas. For several years, Harold W. Luhnow, the then President of the William Volker Charities Fund who had met Hayek in 1945 during *The Road to Serfdom's* promotional lecture tour had urged Hayek to write an American version of the book. Hayek agreed provided he were at an American university. After some discussion, John U. Nef, Chairman of the University of Chicago's Committee on Social Thought, invited Hayek to be Professor of Social and Moral Science. Academic conditions at the Committee on Social Thought were ideal. Relieved of his administrative duties, which had become quite substantial by the time he left the LSE, and only having to teach if and when he chose,

Hayek was able to indulge his catholic interests in social and political theory. This new freedom was reflected in his publications from this period. After publishing numerous papers on economic and social theory from the 1930s and 1940s as *Individualism and Economic Order* in 1948, 1951 saw the publication of a book on J. S. Mill's letters enti-tled *John Stuart Mill and Harriet Taylor: Their Friendship and Subsequent Marriage*. Thereafter, in 1952 Hayek published a study on the method-ology of social science entitled *The Counter-Revolution of Science: Studies in the Abuse of Reason*. A central preoccupation of this book, which had emerged from a series of papers written in the early 1940's, was the question of methodology in the natural and social sciences. Hayek's argument was that natural science methodology had been imitated by the social scientists, including the economists, and that this had lead to 'scientism' in which the theoretical capacity to explain, predict and control social processes is exaggerated. In addition, Hayek's work on theoretical psychology, that had commenced life as the 1920s research paper on consciousness, was taken up again at the end of World War II, and finally published in 1952 as *The Sensory Order*. At this time Hayek also continued to be involved in the more direct promotion of liberal ideas, being instrumental in the founding in London of the Institute of Economic Affairs in 1955, the free-market think tank that later inspired Thatcherism.

Hayek's work on J. S. Mill's correspondence also inspired what became one of his most well-known books when in 1954 he secured funding from the Guggenheim Foundation to retrace the tour that Mill made to Italy and Greece between the winter of 1854 and the spring of 1855. Importantly, and given that he was able to travel much faster than Mill, Hayek also had time to give a series of invited lectures on liberalism in Cairo in celebration of the Bank of Egypt's fiftieth anniversary. After publishing these lectures in 1955 as *The Political Ideal of the Rule of Law* Hayek's intention was to use this material as a basis for a fuller investigation of the themes they explored. Thus emerged the idea to write two books on the liberal order, the first volume of which was to be *The Constitution of Liberty*. He worked on this book for the next four years, completing it on his sixtieth birthday. Timed to coin-cide with the one hundredth anniversary of the publication of Mill's *On Liberty, The Constitution of Liberty* was published in February 1960 and developed many of the ideas that he had previously explored as an economist about the importance of liberal institutions to the effec-tive communication and use of social knowledge. Noteworthy, too, was

Hayek's addition to his thought of the ideas of tradition and of cultural evolution as essential aspects of what he understood to be liberalism's core epistemological function. Despite this, Hayek was disappointed by *The Constitution of Liberty*'s reception as it had did not prove to be as popular as *The Road to Serfdom* had been some 15 years before.

Europe 1962–1992

After the William Volker Charities Fund was dissolved in April 1962, Hayek feared that his Chicago salary would be cut off. Mindful of this and that he would only receive a single lump sum payment upon retiring at 65, Hayek accepted an offer to teach in Germany. Thus, in the autumn of that year Hayek left Chicago to become Professor of Economic Policy at the University of Freiburg, where he stayed until his retirement in 1968. Accepting the offer at Freiburg did come with conditions, not least that he had to return to teaching economics. Despite this, Hayek was able to find the time to concentrate on his central areas of interest: political and legal theory, as well as political economy. It was during this productive period in Freiburg between 1962 and 1969 that Hayek's *magnum opus, Law, Legislation and Liberty,* was mostly written. Published in three volumes in 1973, 1976 and 1979 this book is in many ways the summation of Hayek's intellectual journey where the themes which had preoccupied him over the previous half century coalesced into a single work. Much of his other work from this time was also published in a collection of essays from the 1960s on a wide variety of subjects, appropriately entitled *Studies in Philosophy, Politics and Economics.*

Having officially retired the year before, in 1969 Hayek became honorary Professor of Political Economy at the University of Salzburg in his native Austria. His time there, however, was not a particularly fruitful one, not least because the university did not confer doctoral degrees in the social sciences, thus limiting the number of serious students of economics, and because academics had to inform the government of travel abroad lasting more than eight days. Soon after arriving Hayek entered a period of deep depression which gravely inhibited his output. Whilst lasting until 1973, his condition had improved when, in 1974, he unexpectedly shared the Nobel Memorial Prize in Economics, causing a revival of interest in the Austrian School. Perhaps surprisingly, the last years of Hayek's career saw not only a reinvigorated output, but also a return to economics, culminating in the publication in 1976 by the Institute of Economic Affairs of his *Denationalisation of Money*. Here he argued against governmental monopoly of the provision of money as a means of avoiding cyclical bouts of recession – a topic which, in the wake of the credit crisis that occurred at the conclusion of the first decade of the twenty-first century, has come once more to occupy an important place in discussion about the respective roles of the state and the market. Having decided to leave Salzburg, Hayek returned to Freiburg in 1977 and a year later published a second volume of collected essays written between the late 1960s and mid-1970s entitled *New Studies in Philosophy, Politics, Economics and the History of Ideas*.

The highpoint of Hayek's influence on politics came in the 1970s as think-tanks sympathetic to the pro-market position of what came to be called the New Right emerged throughout the industrialized world. His ideas were also adopted by Margaret Thatcher who helped to set up the Centre for Policy Studies in 1974, a Conservative Party think-tank with a policy agenda that was sympathetic to Hayek's philosophical stance and which proved to be the source of many of the policies adopted by her as Prime Minister following the 1979 general election.[11] In 1984, on the advice of Thatcher, Hayek was appointed as a member of the Order of the Companions of Honour by Queen Elizabeth II for his services to the study of economics. Subsequent to the onset of ill-health from mid-1985 onwards, Hayek's output decreased markedly. Nevertheless, in 1991 President George H. W. Bush awarded Hayek with the Presidential Medal of Freedom, one of the two highest civilian awards in the United States. After a prolonged period of ill-health, Hayek died on 23 March 1992 in Freiburg, Germany. He is buried in the Neustift am Wald cemetery outside of Vienna.

Notes

[1] Hayek, F. A., *Hayek on Hayek: An Autobiographical Dialogue*, in Kresge, S. and Wenar, L. (eds), London, Routledge, 1994, p. 48.

[2] Hayek, F. A., 'Beiträge zur Theorie der Entwicklung des Bewusstseins', Heim, G. (trans.), Hoover Institution, Hayek Archives, Box 92, Folder 1, 1920.

[3] Hayek, *Hayek on Hayek*, p. 67.

[4] Hayek, F. A., 'Foreword', in Mises, L. (ed.), *Socialism: And Economic ad Sociological Analysis*, 1922 (1981), Indianapolis, Liberty Classics, 1981, p. xix.

[5] Ibid.

[6] Machlup and Haberler became economists, Vogelin a political philosopher. Kaufmann and Schutz were philosophers working in phenomenology, the former also being a member of the Vienna Circle. Morgenstern became one of the pioneers of Game Theory.

[7] Steele, G. R., *Keynes and Hayek: The Money Economy*, London, Routledge, 2001, p. 9.

[8] Quoted in Ebenstein, A., *Friedrich Hayek: A Biography*, Chicago, IL, University of Chicago Press, 2001, p. 84.

[9] Ibid., pp. 156–157.

[10] Finer, H., *The Road to Reaction*, Boston, MA, Little Brown and Co., 1945.

[11] Cockett, R., Thinking the Unthinkable: Think-Tanks and the Economic Counter-Revolution 1931–1983, New York, NY, Harper Collins, 1995.

2

Epistemology and Social Theory

Mind and the Sensory Order

Subjectivism and psychology

As we saw in the previous chapter, Hayek's views on mind were first set out in an early research paper that he had written in the 1920s. However, it is only in his book *The Sensory Order* and in some of the papers that followed that what has come to be called Hayek's 'connectionist' theory of mind appears in its most complete form.[1] It is also noteworthy that many of the themes permeating his thought in other disciplines, both prior and subsequent to the publication of this study, are in evidence. For this reason we need to begin our investigation of Hayek's thought with his theory of mind. To be sure, it will not be our purpose to critically evaluate Hayek's theory in any exhaustive way. Rather, by setting out what is a complex and sometimes difficult theory, we will introduce some of the principal strands of Hayek's thought which, along with his unfolding, ever-widening research project, ultimately extended into areas far beyond theoretical psychology. These are the themes of 1) the methodological importance of subjective mental states, 2) our propensity for rule-governed behaviour, 3) tacit knowledge, 4) spontaneous order and evolution, and 5) of the nature and limits of human reason.[2]

Hayek commences his investigation of mind by distinguishing between what he calls the 'physical' or 'natural' order and the 'phenomenal' or 'sensory' order. The first is comprised of the everyday objects and events of the world and of the relationships between them which are investigated via the methods of scientific enquiry. In contrast, the subjectively experienced phenomenal or sensory order is this physical world *as it is apprehended by our senses*. This distinction is crucial to understanding Hayek's purposes for the problem that he seeks to address in *The Sensory Order* is why our phenomenal picture does not always accord with how the world actually is, as revealed by science. This occurs in instances when two different substances – for example, sugar and salt – appear to our senses as physically similar (in this case to our vision) and, conversely, when the same substance affects our senses in different ways, as in the case of lemon juice when applied to the tongue or to the eyes.[3]

This occasional discrepancy is significant for Hayek because it explains why our beliefs about the world sometimes prove to be unfounded, for example when we mistakenly sweeten a cup of tea with salt. More profoundly, however, it clarifies the differing tasks of natural science and of theoretical psychology and introduces the idea of the methodological importance of subjective mental states, which we will see later is fundamentally significant not just to Hayek's theory of mind. Scientific enquiry's principal task, Hayek says, is 'to replace the classification of events which our senses perform, but which proves inadequate to describe the regularities in these events, by a classification which will put us in a better position to do so'.[4] In contrast, theoretical psychology's aim is to explain *why* this discrepancy occurs in the first place. That is, whilst the discrepancy between the natural order and the sensory order means that science is minded to *replace* our mental ordering of the physical world with an objective one that enables us to make our way through it more successfully, theoretical psychology is a *subjective* science in the sense that it is concerned precisely with that which finds 'no place in the account of that world which the physical sciences give us'.[5] Despite the occasional inaccuracy of this subjective representation, it is to it that we must look, and not to scientifically established objective properties and relations, if we are to understand mind. Theoretical psychology, then, tells us something quite different to physical science: not whether our mental or sensory reproduction of the objects of the world and of the relationships between those objects is correct, but rather how that reproduction is often at odds with the objective picture that science provides.

Mind as classificatory system of sensory relations

How, then, is the physical order transformed into the sensory order? Here Hayek assumes the standard account of the structure of the central nervous system where this transformation is performed.[6] Central to this process is the cerebral cortex, the part of the brain responsible for functions such as perceptual awareness, thought, memory, language and consciousness. The cerebral cortex is comprised of up to 100 billion excitable cells, or neurons, that process and transmit information by electrochemical signalling and serves as a bridge between *afferent* fibres that conduct impulses *from* receptor organs to the central nervous system, and *efferent* fibres that conduct impulses from the central nervous system *to* motor organs, so that we can move and perform other bodily functions. Each neuron is in turn connected to approximately 7,000 neighbouring neurons by specialized junctions called synapses, of which there are thought to be between 100 and 500 *trillion* in an adult human brain. It is through them that neurons signal to each other, as well as to *non*-neuronal cells such as those in muscles or glands. It is important to note that the sensory experiences that the brain processes are generally not singular events. Rather, they are comprised of multiple impulses originating from stimuli that tend to occur together, which correspond to the various aspects of the observed object(s) or event(s), and which are transmitted by several neighbouring receptors in the sensory organ concerned. The transmission of these multiple impulses creates connective pathways, or 'linkages', between neurons, owing to the fact that prior travelling along the same part of the neural network by similar impulses makes it more likely that future similar impulses will flow more easily through those pathways. Given the vast number of neurons and synapses involved in this process, the potential number and complexity of connective patterns that can be built up between them in the network is similarly vast.

Hayek claims that this standard view of the physical-to-mental transformative process asserts that the mind is a repository for sense data transmitted via sensory fibres and stored in nerve cells. These data are said to represent or correspond to objects in the external world and 'are supposed to form the raw material which the mind accumulates and learns to arrange in various manners' so that it may constantly adapt itself to its environment.[7] This is called the 'storage' theory of the mind in which 'with every experience some new mental entity representing sensations or images enters the mind or the brain and is there retained until it is returned at the appropriate moment'.[8] In terms of the specific physiological process by which these pure sense data come to be stored in this way, the storage view asserts that it is the *unique* nature of the process of transmission along the nerve fibres which determines the specific nature of the sensation that follows. Thus, the redness and hardness of an apple is transmitted to the central nervous system as 'redness' and 'hardness' in virtue of the physical dissimilarity of those transmissions from those which occur when, for example, the properties of a soft blue object are transmitted. Hayek, however, rejects this view. Rather, he claims that 'sensory...qualities are not in some manner originally attached to, or an original attribute of, the individual physiological impulses'.[9] This view, he claims, cannot explain how these data are coherent to us, especially as, subsequent to being stimulated, receptor organs transmit physically *indistinguishable* electrochemical impulses to the central nervous system which end up being significant to the organism in different ways, depending on the kind of initial stimulus.[10] There is for Hayek, then, no one-to-one correspondence between physical properties and sensory qualities, and mind is not a passive storehouse of brute and unique perceptual data.

In his view it is the *place* that the pathways of stimulated neurons occupy in the whole network, and not on the basis of the unique properties of any impulse, that determines the phenomenal significance of the object or event for us.[11] On this reading, rather than viewing mental phenomena as entities that are caused by the external world, it is '[t]he *connections* between the physiological elements' that are 'the primary phenomenon which creates the mental phenomena' that is significant to us.[12] 'The qualities which we attribute to the experienced objects,' that is, are 'not properties of objects at all, but a set of relations by which our nervous system classifies them'.[13] The operation of mind is thus a process in which stimuli are discriminated, transformed and grouped, with stimuli belonging to the same class if they provoke the same response. As the psychologist Heinrich Klüver wrote in the Introduction to *The Sensory Order,*

> [w]hat we perceive are never unique properties of individual objects, but always only properties which the objects have in common with other objects. Perception is thus always an interpretation, the placing of something into one or several classes of objects.[14]

The role of rules in Hayek's theory of mind

This connectionist rather than storage view of mind can be objected to on at least two grounds. Firstly, it does not explain how perception ever commences. If mind is nothing more than a classificatory mechanism based on the establishment of neural connections between kinds of stimuli, then it needs to have some means of inititating the process of classification so that the world may start to be meaningful. The problem here is that when the mind experiences the world for the first time, it will not be able to perceive anything at all if its capacity to do so is only constituted by previous classifications. In a manner reminiscent of Immanuel Kant's postulation of inherent mental categories which impress order upon the objects of our sensory experience, Hayek addresses this concern by positing what he calls a set of pre-sensory linkages hardwired into our nervous system and which 'is not *learned* by sensory experience, but is rather *implicit* in the means through which we obtain such experience'.[15] He assumes that the elementary structure of the central nervous system is already in place at, or soon after, conception and that the connections created in the neural network are only formed afterwards during the course of our lifetime. There are, therefore, both species-based, or 'phylogenetic', and individual, or 'ontogenetic' factors that explain our capacity to classify the elements of the environment in which we find ourselves as belonging to one or another class of phenomena.

The relationship between these phylogenetic and ontogenetic factors is also relevant to a second objection, Hayek's response to which introduces the second important theme that we will see permeates his thought elsewhere. Given the central importance of mental states to his subjectivist, methodology, Hayek needs to explain how we can interpret the mental processes of other people, or even be sure that they undergo mental processes at all. In epistemology and the philosophy of mind, this is known as the problem of 'other minds'. Its significance arises from the fact that an individual only has direct access to his *own* thoughts, thus leaving unexplained the grounds upon which he can attribute intelligible mental processes to others. In a fashion reminiscent of the argument from analogy to be found in J. S. Mill, Bertrand Russell and A. J. Ayer, Hayek responds to this problem in the first instance by claiming that the reactions of other people to external stimuli are, just like our own perceptions of the world, *themselves* stimuli which our minds classify.[16] Thus, just as we learn to classify stimuli in virtue of how they impact upon our senses, so we learn through the experience of classifying other people's responses that they generally classify in the same way, as for example, when seen to grimace as we do at the taste of tea sweetened with salt.[17] Moreover, it is here that the idea of *language* becomes significant for Hayek locates this broad similarity across different individuals in the very possibility of *intelligible conversation* about our classifications. It would simply not be possible, he contends, to have the meaningful conversations we can and do have about the world unless there was a significant degree of phylogenetic, species-based commonality in the way in which we classify our experiences of it.

Hayek elaborates on our common capacity to classify by introducing the idea of our perception and action being *rule-guided*.[18] To be sure, when using the term 'rule' he does not want to claim that it refers to something in any physical sense. Rather, by 'rule' Hayek means the regularity and orderliness with which mental and motor processes occur. Rules are important for at least two reasons. Firstly, they explain the orderliness of our own experience of and behaviour in the world. It is because our perception is rule-guided that we do not experience the world as but a chaotic flux of random disparate events but rather classify and thus make sense of it. Similarly to our capacity for rule-guided perception, moreover, Hayek also discusses our propensity for rule-guided action, such as our capacity to use the rules of grammar when speaking a language, as explaining why we also act in an orderly fashion. Importantly, rules not only explain the regularity of our actions, but also delimit the range of available options open to us in any given situation. Thus, for Hayek it is our perception or rule-guided subjective 'interpretation' of the world that determines our action in it. The rule-guided manner in which we order our experience of the world, that is, is the ultimate determinant of our response to that world and it is this which constitutes our ability to adapt to our environment successfully.[19]

Equally significantly for his response to the problem of other minds, Hayek also claims that rule-guided perception and action also explain how the experience of *others* is similar to ours and that we are capable of interpreting it as such. The fact that we perceive according to rules explains, for example, our capacity to understand one another's utterances as language and not noise, or others' actions as fitting into a coherent system or 'pattern', rather than as a chaotic sequence of bewildering perceptual events. For Hayek, then, it is because of our own rule-guided capacity to perceive and act that renders the actions of others as *meaningful* or, as he puts it, 'intelligible', to us. The very possibility of the meaningfulness of the actions of others and, more significantly for his wider purposes, of *their inner thoughts and beliefs* being meaningful to us when they express them through language, or other cultural media such as art, is because of our common propensity to perceive and act in similar ways under relevantly similar circumstances.[20]

Imitative learning and tacit knowledge

This regulative commonality is borne out in a particularly vivid way by our capacity to correct, learn from and imitate one another. The most obvious example of this is our capacity to imitate *speech*. It is a particularly straightforward example, Hayek suggests, because 'the sounds emitted by an individual are perceived by him as similar to those produced by another'.[21] More difficult to explain, however, if not via the notion of rule-guided perception and action, is our capacity to imitate the *physical movements* of others. Unlike speech, in the case of physical movements there is no direct correspondence between the actions we perceive others to undertake and the perception of our own actions, because 'the movements of one's own body are perceived in a manner altogether different from that in which the corresponding movements of another person are perceived'.[22] Yet, significantly, this is no obstacle to successful imitation, most obviously, in our ability to learn and copy new skills from one another. It is the possibility of imitative learning, then, that not only provides us with the evidence that we act and perceive on a rule-guided basis, but that others do so, too and that these rules are held in common with them. This is significant because it suggests that lying behind Hayek's subjectivism is an *intersubjective* stance. He writes as follows:

> [A]lthough the system of sensory qualities is 'subjective' in the sense of belonging to the perceiving subject as distinguished from 'objective' (belonging to the perceived objects) – a distinction which is the same as that between the phenomenal and physical order, it is yet interpersonal and not (or at least not entirely) peculiar to the individual.[23]

The examples of language and skills are also significant to Hayek as examples of a more general phenomenon which can be described as our propensity to have 'know-how' or 'tacit' knowledge and which we will see figures in his work in other disciplines. Importantly for Hayek, and in contrast to our explicit or propositional knowledge – for example, our knowledge of facts about the world – the knowledge involved in our knowing how, to speak a language, engage in arts and crafts, or play tennis, is knowledge which we are either unable, or do not need, to articulate in order for it to be utilized efficaciously.[24] Moreover, we are generally unable to specify in any detail how we are able to imitate the complex of elements that we classify and combine to reproduce a skill learnt from another person, not only because they are far too numerous for us to list, but also because our knowledge of them is often subconscious.[25] Similarly, Hayek emphasizes that we are generally unable, or do not need, to explain why we know that an utterance or action is not in conformity with the rules that govern the phenomenon of which it is a part, in order for corrective learning to be successful. Again, this is because the knowledge involved in doing so is largely tacit in nature and, as such, of a non-articulable form.

Maps, models and the theory of spontaneous order

We have seen that science shows how our subjective picture of the world can be mistaken, and that this fact is central to Hayek's theoretical psychology. Yet, it is not only science which shows us that we often err in this regard. Our own first-hand experience of ourselves and of others as beings who seek, and sometimes fail, to make their way successfully in the world also confirms this in a particularly direct manner. Importantly, we have also seen that it is from this occasional disappointment of our expectations that we constantly learn to reclassify the objects and events of the world. Along, then, with the rule-guided perception and action that for Hayek are at the core of this process, of equal importance are his concepts of the mind's phenomenal *map* and of the temporary *models* it forms of the world as a result of its operation.[26] Most significantly, it is the nature of the relationship between these two phenomena that introduces the fourth major theme permeating Hayek's wider intellectual enterprise: that of the spontaneous ordering process.

The mind's map just is the totality of neural connections made by travelling impulses that are established through the course of a person's lifetime. Importantly, this map is said to be relatively static in that it does not provide any information about the environment in which we find ourselves at any given moment. It represents, rather, 'the kind of world in which the organism has existed in the past, or the different kinds of stimuli which have acquired significance for it' and 'provides the framework within which the impulses proceeding at any time are evaluated'.[27] The mind's map, of course, will only ever amount to an approximation of the objective objects, events and relationships of the world it classifies and often is an erroneous one.[28] Precisely because of this, the map is also said to be transformed over time in the light of our experience and for this reason Hayek calls it 'semi-permanent'. The fact of the map's semi-permanent nature is important because it explains the significance of the idea of what Hayek calls the temporary models that are formed in the mind at any given moment. In contrast to the relatively static overall framework that is the map, by a 'model' Hayek refers to that part of the neural network that is stimulated by, and thus representative of, the world at any given moment, depending on the specific pathways the stimuli that provoke it travel upon. The model thus draws from the map to represent the 'particular environment in which the organism finds itself at the moment and which will enable it to take account of that environment in all of its movement'.[29] Importantly, whenever there occurrs a new experience represented by a model that is inconsistent with the mind's map formed thus far, it is the map that is revised. Thus, in a case where we experience a white substance hitherto classified as sugar, but which turns out to be salt when tasted, the configuration of neural connections in the map which comprise our subjective, sensory experience of these substances, is altered.[30]

The relationship between the temporary models and the semi-permanent map of accumulated linkages, therefore, is a corrective and transformative one that enables the organism to adapt itself to its environment. This is greatly significant for Hayek because it suggests that the process by which we adapt to our environment over the course of our lifetime is driven by discrete events of model-based validation and invalidation, or learning. That is, rather than being the result of a deliberate process of selection, the map is the *emergent* outcome of a *spontaneous* process. The adaptations to the environment the mind effects, that is, are not directed from a central point, but rather are the results of internal model-driven reconfigurations. Equally significantly, and given that our minds are constantly undergoing this transformative process within the context of our different ongoing personal experiences and, perhaps most fundamentally, the different anatomical structures of our bodies that determine the specific quality of our sensory experience, the personal knowledge of the world that is spontaneously built up in this way inevitably differs from one individual to another.[31]

The complexity of mind and the limits of reason

The fact that the mind's map develops in this spontaneous manner is also significant for Hayek insofar as it introduces a fifth theme in his *oeuvre:* that of the nature and limits of our capacity to explain and predict spontaneously-emergent phenomena. Firstly, and given that the sensory order of mind itself is a spontaneously evolving entity, Hayek argues that, unlike branches of the natural sciences, that deal with relatively simple phenomena such as physics, our powers of explanation of mind can only ever be limited to an *explanation of the principle* by which it operates.

In the first instance, this is because the number of variables relevant to the determination of the map is simply too great for a human mind to manipulate.[32] However, it is not just for such relatively obvious computational reasons that we can only ever give an explanation of the principle, rather than of the detail, of the formation of the sensory order. There is, also, a predictive obstacle. Given that we cannot know in advance which particular experiences we will have, we are never in a position to exhaustively list all the sensory experiences we would need to list in order to predict the future development of the mind successfully. In addition, given that a significant aspect of this spontaneous process involves our perception of the actions of *others*, we could never actually list all the determinants of our own mind's map of the world without doing the same for them. It is, then, this fundamentally reciprocal influence and intersubjectivity of the spontaneous evolution of individual minds upon one another that, for Hayek, means that we could only ever give an explanation of the principle rather than of the detail of the formation of the mind's map. Fourthly, there is the fact discussed earlier that much of what we know is of a practical or tacit nature. The consequence of this is that many of the mentally transformative experiences we have are themselves founded upon the perception of actions whose motivation we cannot fully explain. Finally, because in the case of mind the *quaesitum*, or object, of explanation is also the entity employed to give that explanation, we are unavoidably limited in our powers to do so. 'No explaining agent', Hayek writes, 'can ever explain objects of its own kind, or of its own degree of complexity, and, therefore...the human brain can never fully explain its own operations'.[33]

Nevertheless, and given that the formation of the sensory order of mind is ultimately accounted for by the physiology of the central nervous system, it would seem reasonable to conclude that Hayek's theory is a thoroughgoing materialist one. Yet, if this is the case, Hayek has a problem, for it also stands to reason that he is wrong to think that mind cannot be fully explained. If, after all, mind is reducible to discrete neural events, then it must in principle be possible for it to be explained in terms of them. However, precisely because of the complex relationship of the mind to the physical order it seeks to comprehend, Hayek would reject this view and his stance is more accurately described as a non-reductive physicalism or, in his own terms, a 'practical' rather than principled dualism. That is, despite ultimately being determined by physical events, the nature of the process by which they are transformed into the sensory order of mind means that mind itself is irreducible to a description of those events. As Hayek explains towards the end of *The Sensory Order*,

> [t]he conclusion to which our theory leads is thus that to us not only mind as a whole but also all individual mental processes must forever remain phenomena of a special kind which, although produced by the same principles which we know to operate in the physical world, we shall never be able to fully explain in terms of physical laws. Those whom it pleases may express this by saying that in some ultimate sense mental phenomena are 'nothing but' physical processes; this, however, does not alter the fact that in discussing mental processes we will never be able to dispense with the use of mental terms, and that we shall have permanently to be content with a practical dualism, a dualism based not on any assertion of an objective difference between the two classes of events, but on the demonstrable limitations of the powers of our own mind to fully comprehend the unitary order to which they belong.[34]

It follows, he concludes, that we will never be able to achieve a 'complete unification of all sciences in the sense that all phenomena of which it treats can be described in physical terms' and it is in this fundamental sense that subjective mental states will always have to be taken as given.[35]

Despite these clear limits to explanation, at no point does Hayek claim that we cannot derive *any* useful knowledge from our study of complex spontaneous processes similar to that found in the case of the development of the mind. What we can do in the face of such complexity, of course, is to explain the principle by which the mind works and this is precisely what Hayek's connectionist theory sets out to do. Importantly, moreover, we should not feel discouraged by the fact that, with respect to some phenomena, an explanation of the principle is all that we can give. Whilst, for instance, being incapable of performing the most complex mathematical tasks ourselves, our knowledge of the principles of mathematics and of design enables us to construct machines which can. Of course, precisely because we cannot perform the calculations that such machines perform, we are never in a position to absolutely verify that the specific results they give are actually correct. Yet it would be unreasonable to claim that because of this shortcoming we should not make use of the calculations yielded. Instead we relax the criterion of correctness to one of being in conformity with the principles by which the calculating machine operates, and not with our knowledge of whether a specific result is correct. Indeed, the efficacy of our employing the calculations of machines in areas such as avionics suggests that explanations of the principle are both verifiable and have beneficial consequences. By contrast, for Hayek, adhering strictly to an explanation of the detail as the relevant criterion of acceptability, would mean, in the case of complex phenomena, that we achieve far less than a more judicious use of reason would permit. This, we will see throughout this book, is a point to which he returns repeatedly in his economic and political theory.[36]

Social Theory and The Knowledge Problem

Subjectivism and social science

It is not just in his theoretical psychology that Hayek claims that adequate understanding necessitates the investigation of our subjective, sensory ordering of the world rather than of its objective physical properties as established by scientific enquiry. By a similar logic, in the closing passages of *The Sensory Order* he seeks to establish the methodological importance of subjective mental states when claiming that natural science method is also inapplicable to the study of our *social* world.[37] The reason for this is that 'only what people know or believe can enter as a motive into their conscious action', even if these beliefs are actually false according to science.[38] Moreover and as we have seen he emphasised in his theoretical psychology, the determinants of these beliefs are in any case irreducible to objective properties:

[e]ven though we may know the general principle by which all human action is causally determined by physical processes, this would not mean that to us a particular human action can ever be recognizable as the necessary result of a particular set of physical circumstances. To us, human decisions must always appear as the result of the whole of a human personality – that means the whole of a person's mind – which, as we have seen, we cannot reduce to something else.[39]

Because of this, what we believe, Hayek adds, 'must be regarded as a significant datum of experience' not only in the study of mind. For Hayek it is also 'the starting point in any discussion' of human behaviour.[40] Thus, whereas in theoretical psychology we need to adopt a subjectivist stance in order to understand why our perception of the material world is often revealed to be incorrect, and the beliefs we form upon the basis of those perceptions are sometimes disappointed, in social theory subjectivism is important as a device for understanding the consequences of our acting upon those beliefs. The question of the explanation of purposive human action is one that Hayek takes up in more detail in *The Counter-Revolution of Science*, as well as in 'The Facts of the Social Sciences' where he is concerned 'with the common character of all disciplines which deal with the results of conscious human action'.[41] Significantly, and to further attest to the underlying unity of his thought, we will see that Hayek's social theory exhibits other commonalities and continuities with his theory of mind. To be sure, this is not to say that he says nothing new here. In his most enduring contribution to twentieth-century thought, Hayek's social theory also witnesses the explicit working out of his idea about the special nature of social knowledge in complex societies and of the 'Knowledge Problem' that this presents to them.

Hayek first applies his subjectivist method with respect to what he calls individual social facts. These include socially significant objects such as tools, as well as acts such as greeting, warning, producing or exchanging. In stark contrast to the method of the natural sciences where it is precisely upon physical properties that attention is focused, in the social sciences tools and socially significant acts are social facts from which the social theorist abstracts away *all* physical properties for the purposes of understanding. 'Whether a medicine is a medicine, *for the purposes of understanding a person's actions*', Hayek writes, 'depends solely on whether the person believes it to be one, irrespective of whether we, the observers, agree or not', or whether the person is actually mistaken in their belief . 'In short', he explains, 'in the social sciences the things are what people think they are', independently of the beliefs of the observer, or of the findings of science.[42] To be sure, this is not to say that socially significant human actions and tools, devices and instruments are not, similar to the phenomena that are of interest to natural science, objective in the sense of being independent of the observer. After all, what the social scientist studies 'is not determined by his fancy or imagination'. Yet, 'in another sense', Hayek continues, these social facts 'do differ from the facts of the physical sciences in being beliefs or opinions held by particular people, beliefs which as such are our data, irrespective of whether they are true or false'.[43]

Similar to the argument made in *The Sensory Order*, the necessity of adopting this subjectivist stance is brought out when we seek to explain why, for example, an agent treats what are entirely different physical objects in the same way, as is the case in the use of money in its different forms. Clearly a shell, a coin and a five pound note share few, if any, physical properties in common. Yet despite this they are in an important sense examples of the same object even though the acting person perceives them as physically dissimilar. The reason for this, of course, has little to do with their physical properties at all but, rather, with what the agent takes them to mean or signify.[44] Thus despite the often reverential nature of our attitude to natural science method, adopting such an approach with respect to social phenomena would leave the social scientist incapable of accounting for people's actions. Far from being a superior method to be emulated, the adoption of natural science method with respect to individual social facts would, for Hayek, result in explanatory failure.[45]

Even if he has established the importance of agents' subjective mental states to our understanding of their actions, Hayek is sensitive to the question of the confidence with which the observing social scientist may make claims about their beliefs and attitudes.[46] Similar to his response to the problem of other minds in his theoretical psychology, Hayek claims that it is because the meaning we attribute to individual social facts is shared with those we observe that, in the social sciences, we are able to classify such facts as similar. That is, we can recognize the underlying beliefs and attitudes from what those we study 'do and say merely because we have ourselves a mind similar to theirs'.[47] Indeed, the fact of this commonality 'must necessarily precede and is presupposed by any communication with other men' and 'is shown

not merely by the possibility of communicating with other people –
we act on this knowledge every time we speak or write; it is confirmed
by the very results of our study of the external world'.[48]

To be sure, the commonality which Hayek has in mind is not only
the phylogenetic set of rules of perception and action, but also that of
the shared cultural or conventional rules that define meaningfulness.
The necessity of assuming the truth of this intersubjective commonality is made all the more clear when we analyse purposive behaviour in
cultures different to our own. Indeed, it is this fact, Hayek claims, that
explains why, when the

> possibility of interpreting in terms of analogies from our own mind
> ceases, where we can no longer 'understand', there is no sense in
> speaking about mind at all; there are then only physical facts which
> we can group and classify solely according to the physical properties
> which we observe.[49]

Just as was the case with his theory of mind, then, Hayek's social
theory is *au fond* an intersubjectivist one that places him in a tradition of thought that includes his *Geistkreis* colleague Schutz, Edmund
Husserl, Maurice Merleau-Ponty, G. H. Mead and, most recently,
Jurgen Habermas.[50]

The theory of spontaneous social order

Importantly, the classification of subjective knowledge, beliefs and
attitudes is not done to account for individual social facts for their
own sake. Of greater interest to Hayek is how the actions undertaken
as a consequence of our having this knowledge play a role in the
emergence of an altogether different type of social phenomenon in
which 'by his actions, determined by the views and concepts he pos-
sesses, man builds up another world of which the individual becomes a
part'.[51] Indeed, Hayek adds somewhat cryptically, '[w]hile science is all
the time busy revising the picture of the external world that man pos-
sesses, and while to it this picture is always provisional,' he writes, 'the
fact that man *has* a definite picture, and that the picture of all beings
whom we recognize as thinking men and whom we can understand is
to some extent alike, is no less a reality of great consequence' and is
'the *cause* of certain events' which social science needs to explain.[52]

What could Hayek mean by this? Key here is the insight that precisely because our minds are rule-governed and classify the world in similar ways, we also respond to that world by acting in similar ways under relevantly similar circumstances, as the earlier example of our common propensity to grimace at the taste of poorly prepared tea made clear. Importantly, though, this commonality does not only explain behavioural similarities and regularities across different individuals with respect to responses to external stimuli. It also explains how, under relevantly similar conditions, individuals behave in such ways as to induce the formation of coherent and intelligible social structures *that emerge independently of their specific intentions*. At first glance, this is quite a difficult concept to grasp, so it will be useful here to give some examples in order to clarify the underlying logic of the idea. Most obviously, as we have seen, Hayek's own example of the spontaneous formation of the mind's semi-permanent map is an example of this kind of phenomenon. In the non-human natural world a particularly useful and striking example of the logic of this phenomenon is that of *allelomimesis*, or the manner in which the individual movements of, for instance, birds or fish give the appearance of the flock or shoal within which each moves as having a mind of its own, particularly seen to respond as a single entity when under attack from a predator. Of course, there is neither a group mind nor, for that matter, a leader co-coordinating the flock or shoal. Rather each animal is merely imitating, in rule-guided fashion, the evasive manoeuvres of their neighbours who find themselves closest to danger.[53] An example from human society that exhibits what Hayek calls, quoting historian of economic thought James Bonar, a 'spontaneous social product', is that of the formation of a footpath by different individuals who traverse the same terrain at different times whilst pursuing different purposes.[54] Similar to allelomimesis, Hayek's footpath example is usefully illustrative of the kind of process that he wants to draw our attention to because it points to a physically *observable* entity that emerges independently of the discrete actions of a multiplicity of contributing agents.

Yet, unlike these examples, there also exist logically identical social processes where the resulting whole is *not* observable. It is these which are of most interest to Hayek and which he claims present social science with its principle explanatory task.[55] In the social world such phenomena may occur, for instance, as the result of a long-term process, or as one that is constantly changing over relatively short periods of time. An example of the former would be a language or a moral

code where these are said to be transformed over the long term as a
consequence of the discrete actions of individuals, but which, importantly, do not do so as a result of those individuals' deliberately coordinated, or concerted action. We could also think of the development
of a society's tastes in fashion, cuisine or the arts in a similar manner.
Similarly, Hayek observes, economic theory can show how a myriad
of individuals brings about constant changes in the prices of goods,
without explicitly willing the specific prices that actually emerge. Just
as in the case of allelomimesis, the complex social orders that arise as a
result of this interaction are not said to be the results of the deliberate
concerted action of the several members of society, nor of direction
by an individual or group from the centre. They are, he says, evoking
the idea of Scottish Enlightenment philosopher Adam Ferguson, 'the
results of human action, but not of human design'.[56] Indeed, upon
reflection it soon becomes apparent that, from customs, morals and
law, to language and economics, our social world is replete with such
spontaneous phenomena.[57]

Complexity, *cosmos* and Hayek's Knowledge Problem

From as early as 1935, but especially in the light of the critical response
to *The Counter-Revolution of Science*, Hayek called these spontaneous
social wholes or products 'complex phenomena'.[58] By 'complex'
Hayek meant to describe a characteristic of these phenomena related,
but nonetheless in addition to, their spontaneity. If by their spontaneity he highlighted the manner of the emergence of phenomena
such as prices, language, culture and social order in general, by their
complexity he wished to highlight the fact that this emergence is the
result of the purposive behaviour of more individuals than any single
mind can observe and, as such, is *unavoidably* spontaneous in nature.
That is, precisely because they are complex in this way, such orders
cannot be the result of the self-conscious execution of a plan and can
only emerge spontaneously. This additional characteristic, of course,
meant that Hayek did not assert that all spontaneous orders must be
complex. The relationship between the two features is intransitive, as
is shown by the existence of spontaneously emergent simple orders.
But the important point for Hayek is that, where they *are* so complex as to be beyond our powers of direct observation and deliberate manipulation, such orders must be the results of a spontaneous

process. When writing with reference to society as a whole, Hayek used a special word for this phenomenon, calling the spontaneous order of a complex society a *cosmos*. Moreover, and because it is not the result of the self-conscious execution of a plan, the *cosmos* of society itself cannot be said to have an overall purpose, even if it is serviceable to the purposes of the people of whose rule-guided behaviour it is the unintended result.[59]

Most importantly, and in what is perhaps Hayek's most significant contribution to twentieth century thought, he claims that the knowledge and beliefs of the different people whose actions lead to the formation of complex social order is, 'while possessing that common structure which makes communication possible' also 'different and often conflicting in many respects'.[60] The reason for this in the first instance is because this knowledge is not only *subjective*, but is knowledge of different local circumstances. Most significantly, for Hayek this knowledge is not only therefore unique to the individuals who act upon it, it is the knowledge of individuals who in the overwhelming majority of instances *are not in direct physical contact with one another* and therefore it is knowledge that *can never be given to any single observing mind*. As he claims in *The Counter-Revolution of Science*, this knowledge 'only exists in the dispersed, incomplete, and inconsistent form in which it appears in many individual minds, and the dispersion and imperfection of all knowledge are two of the basic facts from which the social sciences have to start'.[61] In addition, and again as he emphasized in *The Sensory Order*, at least some of these beliefs may not only be subjective in the sense that they are unique to the acting individual, but also in the sense that they can be based upon *misapprehensions*. Most prosaically, this would occur when, believing what turned out to be the *false* rumour that the supply of tea was about to run out, there is a rush on tea that, as if a self-fulfilling prophecy, does indeed affect its availability.

The example of a rush on tea highlights a further characteristic of the phenomenon of complex social order: that of the inescapably social or intersubjective nature of the context within which we act, and in which the character of the circumstances that we have knowledge of is in a non-trivial sense determined by others. The knowledge and beliefs that we have, that is, are not only of local circumstances, they also include our beliefs about the beliefs, attitudes, needs and wants of others. Thus, just as in his theory of mind intersubjectivity meant that an exhaustive account of why we have the beliefs we have could never be given, for Hayek it is similarly impossible to give such a complete account of the knowledge that helps to determine our actions, as doing so would involve doing the same for everybody else. Finally, and given the importance he attaches to tacit knowledge and know-how, for Hayek this subjective knowledge that is one of the determinants of the actions that we undertake is non-articulable. 'Though our civilization is the result of a cumulation of individual knowledge', he writes,

> it is not by their explicit or conscious combination of all this knowledge in any individual brain, but by its embodiment in symbols which we use without understanding them, in habits and institutions, tools and concepts, that man in society is constantly able to profit from a body of knowledge neither he nor any other man completely possesses. Many of the greatest things man has achieved are the result not of consciously directed thought, and still less the product of a deliberately coordinated effort of many individuals, but of a process in which the individual plays a part which he can never fully understand.[62]

This fact of the subjective, dispersed, socially constituted and 'tacit' nature of the unique and sometimes erroneous motivating beliefs relevant to the formation of complex social order is deeply significant for Hayek and is the principal *leitmotif* of his entire intellectual enterprise. It is no less than Hayek's Knowledge Problem to which we will see he returns in political, legal and, perhaps most famously, economic theory.

Rules of just conduct and social coordination

Given that there is a Knowledge Problem, how does Hayek say it is solved? How, that is, if the knowledge relevant to the formation of complex social order is never given in its totality to anybody, is it possible that such order nonetheless emerges without central direction? Similarly to his account of the orderliness with which we are able to perceive and act in the world, central to Hayek's answer here is the notion of the rule, or what he calls in his social theory the *rule of just conduct*. Moreover, and again similar to his theory of mind, these rules are not things, but rather *theories* or statements with which we account for regularities in conduct. Rules of just conduct, that is, are said to exist insofar as they are 'honoured in action' when the diverse members of society behave in similar ways under relevantly similar conditions.[63] Moreover, they serve a dual function in Hayek's social theory. Not only does our propensity to follow rules of just conduct explain the emergence of complex social order. The fact that the rules are *shared* also explains how it is possible for that conduct to be coordinated when in the overwhelming majority of circumstances, the acting individuals are not in direct contact with one another. In an important sense, then, our following of common rules of just conduct just is the *solution* to Hayek's Knowledge Problem.

In his social theory Hayek equates the rules of just conduct, with cultural practices and traditions. Thus, starting with *The Political Ideal of the Rule of Law,* Hayek gives an account of how complex social order emerges, even though nobody is ever in a position to bring it about deliberately.[64] '[M]ost of the rules of conduct which govern our actions, and most of the institutions which arise out of this regularity,' he writes, 'are adaptations to the impossibility of anyone taking conscious account of all the particular facts which enter into the order of society.'[65] At the most fundamental level, and similar to his conception of rule-guided action, Hayek claims that the following of rules of just conduct makes social coordination possible without central direction because it delimits the kinds of action that we may undertake in any given situation. Importantly, he notes further this determination is pre-conscious and, indeed, determines the range of choices open to our conscious selection.[66] Moreover, rule-following serves its coordinative function not only by delimiting which actions are appropriate but, equally importantly, which are *not* and it is in this sense that the rules of just conduct are generally prohibitions rather than commands to perform specific actions. Thus, just as our 'scientific' knowledge of cause and effect is useful in helping us avoid sweetening our tea with salt, so Hayek claims that what is in effect our moral knowledge helps us to avoid social danger. 'Taboos or negative rules acting through the paralysing action of fear will', Hayek writes, act 'as a kind of knowledge of what *not* to do' and as such 'constitute just as significant information about the environment as any positive knowledge of the attributes of the objects of this environment'.[67] (The question of whether such taboos are, along with our traditions and practices in general, always fair or just is an important question which Hayek needs to give an answer to and which we will address shortly.)

Most importantly, and just because they delimit our action in this way, the rules of just conduct enable mutually ignorant individuals in large-scale complex societies to coordinate their activities with one another. That is to say rule-following facilitates coordination because it enables actions to be adapted not only to the facts that we do know, that is, those in our immediate environment, but also to those that are located beyond it and known only by unseen others.[68] Key here is the idea of the rules being shared, customary or common. Precisely because others follow similar rules, we are able to anticipate their actions even when they are unseen by us and it is in this sense that Hayek characterizes our following of rules of just conduct as providing us with an 'extrasomatic sense'.[69] Moreover, obeying customary rules of just conduct not only makes social coordination possible between mutually ignorant contemporaries, but also through *time* so that we may take advantage of the experience of previous generations. Rules, then, make possible 'the transmission in time of our accumulated stock of knowledge and the communication among contemporaries of information on which they base their action'.[70]

Given this, it is clear that by rules of just conduct Hayek is giving an account of the coordinative properties of custom, or tradition. Crucially, the knowledge embedded in custom is also largely *tacit* in nature and as such is only made use of through *action*, including by imitation. 'The successful combination of knowledge and aptitude', needed for efficacious social decision-making to take place in a complex society like our own, he writes,

> is the product of individuals imitating those who have been more successful and from their being guided by signs or symbols, such as prices offered for their products or expressions or moral or aesthetic esteem for their having observed standards of conduct – in short, of their using the results of the experiences of others.[71]

What, then, is the precise nature of these rules? This is an important question because it is clear that complex social order would not arise from the following of just any rule or set of rules: a rule of just conduct which mandated the killing of others upon sight would clearly issue in social disorder and breakdown.[72] Hayek describes their specific characteristics in *Rules and Order* where he claims that the rules of just conduct are generally prohibitions which tell us what not to do in a given situation, that they are devoid of reference to specific individuals, roles and responsibilities, and are not command-like in form.[73] The reason for the rules of just conduct possessing these characteristics is intimately related, for Hayek, to their underlying epistemological function. That is, in a society where the vast majority of people are not in direct face-to-face contact, the only way for social order to come about when nobody has access to all the knowledge of local conditions relevant to bringing it about deliberately, is via the free interplay of the agents who have and act upon that knowledge. Hayek captures the distinction at the heart of the rules' function in *The Road to Serfdom* 'as that between laying down a Rule of the Road, as in the Highway Code, and ordering people where to go; or, better still, between providing signposts and commanding people which road to take.'[74] Without this free interplay that non-specific prohibitive rules make possible, that is, complex order simply would not come about. To be sure, and whilst it is possible to consciously improve the overall order the following of rules of just conduct makes possible – what we will see Hayek describes as the self-conscious cultivation of the rules conducive to the achievement of order in a complex society – it is not possible to do so by issuing direct commands. 'We cannot', he writes, 'improve the results by specific commands that deprive its members of the possibility of using their knowledge for their purposes'.[75] Finally, and echoing the importance we have seen he attaches to the idea of tacit knowledge elsewhere, Hayek claims that the rules do not need to be articulated in order to serve their coordinative purpose.[76]

Organization, or *taxis*

Up until this point, the impression may have been given that for Hayek it is only the acting individual who is the principal contributing agent to spontaneous social order. Yet, individuals offten act in organized groups and these are just as important to his account. Importantly, however, the orderliness of the conduct manifested by such groups is itself not spontaneous in nature but rather is the result of intentional design. A particularly useful example of such a non-spontaneous order, or what Hayek calls a *taxis* or organization, is that of a company.[77] Here each employee has a specific role to play and responsibilities that go with that role in furtherance of the predetermined aims of the company. With roles and responsibilities defined in advance, the employees of the company behave in an orderly way in pursuit of its predetermined goals. Whilst themselves non-spontaneous in nature, organizations do nevertheless contribute to the emergence of spontaneous order in society at large and as such play a crucial role in Hayek's social theory.

What, then, of the rules that govern the operation of organizations? At the most basic level, and in contrast to the rules of just conduct, the rules of organization have to be in the form of orders or commands, where specific duties, obligations and responsibilities are explicitly set out. In contrast to the purpose-independent, negative rules of just conduct, the rules of organization are purpose-dependent, command-like and thus are useful in relation to the ultimate aim they serve. Of course, the distinction between rules of just conduct and rules of organization is not meant by Hayek to correspond on a one-to-one basis with *cosmos* and *taxis*. At least in the case of organizations, office-holders also enjoy a significant degree of discretion in determining how they fulfil their duties in furtherance of the wider aims of the organizations of which they are members. The orderliness exhibited in an organization, then, is the result of the following of both kinds of rule.[78] Nevertheless, we can make the distinction between rules of just conduct and rules of organization still clearer by imagining what kind of entity an organization would be if it had an overall purpose, but where the rules that governed it were comprised only of rules of just conduct. Clearly, it could achieve nothing specific at all because the members would have no idea of what they had to do in order to bring the objective about.

Equally importantly, it is in his account of *taxis*, where Hayek introduces a special kind of organization whose primary objective is to ensure the integrity of the spontaneous order of society itself. This need emerges from the fact that, whilst being numerically insignificant compared to the number of occasions where they are honoured in action, *violations* of the rules of just conduct give rise to the need for an alternative mechanism of enforcement when self-enforcement fails. As we will see in Hayek's political theory, this special organization is *the state* and the determination of how it best fulfils this protective role is central to his normative project.[79] Moreover, and just because the state is charged with this specific purpose, it is crucial to Hayek's wider project that he provide an account of the role our *reason* plays in the determination of that role. Given the importance of this task, and therefore before examining Hayek's more specific theory of the state, we need first to look at his account of the role reason plays more generally in explaining spontaneous social order.

Reason and Social Explanation

A communitarian conception of the self

For Hayek, the fact that the knowledge and beliefs relevant to the formation of complex social order is never given in its entirety to a single mind redefines the extent of our powers of social explanation, prediction and control. Thus, just as he made clear in his theoretical psychology, in his social theory Hayek claims that 'in the case of very complex phenomena the powers of science are also limited by the practical impossibility of ascertaining all the particular facts which we would have to know if its theories were to give us the power of predicting specific events'.[80] It is this complexity, moreover, which also explains why, unlike predictions of the outcomes of relatively simple processes, we are necessarily limited in the degree of specificity with which we can make testable claims about complex phenomena. There is a great difference, he notes,

> between the prediction that upon turning a switch the pointer of a measuring instrument will be at a particular figure and the prediction that horses will not give birth to hippogriffs or that, if all commodity prices are fixed by law and demand afterwards increases, people will not be able to buy as much of every commodity as they would wish to buy at these prices.[81]

Yet, numerical complexity is not the only reason for this difficulty. Underlying Hayek's social theory is a theory of human reason which clarifies what he takes to be the proper determination of our power to explain, predict and control spontaneously-emergent complex social phenomena. He initially discusses the nature of human reason under the rubric of a distinction between what he calls 'true' and 'false' individualism. 'True' individualism is in the first instance just another way of describing Hayek's subjectivist and methodologically individualistic method, whose central contention we have seen is that the only way to render the formation of complex social orders intelligible is 'through our understanding of individual actions directed toward other people and guided by their expected behaviour'.[82] Importantly, however, 'true individualism' also refers for Hayek to the idea that these complex social orders are also 'the condition for the achievement of many of the things at which individuals aim, the environment which makes it possible even to conceive of most of our individual desires and which gives us the power to achieve them'.[83] Thus, in the paper 'Individualism: True and False', he is at pains to reject what he calls 'the silliest of common misunderstandings': that individualism 'postulates...the existence of isolated or self-contained individuals' who are endowed with reason independently of the social process. Rather, in a fashion that anticipates later communitarian thought and exhibits some parallels with the work of Judith Butler on the emergence of the moral subject and of the limits of its self-knowledge and capacity to give an account of itself, Hayek claims that 'true' individualism starts with the idea of 'men whose whole nature and character is determined by their existence in society'.[84]

Crucially, he continues, human reason 'does not exist in the singular, as given or available to any particular person,...but must be conceived as an interpersonal process in which anyone's contribution is tested and corrected by the others'.[85] Using the same logic employed in his theory of mind Hayek claims that, similarly to those orders it seeks to understand, an individual's own knowledge is only ever constituted as part of a wider intersubjective or interindividual process in which it finds its content dependent upon circumstances beyond it. Hayek, then, is clearly no social atomist, but rather a thinker for whom mind and society develop concurrently. 'Mind is', he writes in *Rules and Order*, in a passage reminiscent of the account offered in *The Sensory Order*:

> an adaptation to the natural and social surroundings in which man lives and that it has developed in constant interaction with the institutions that determine the structure of society. Mind is as much the product of the social environment in which it has grown up and which it has not made as something that in turn acted upon and altered these institutions.[86]

Given, then, that the mind itself is only ever a product of the very intersubjective process that constitutes the social order it seeks to explain, it would be impossible for it to give a complete account of that order, as this would presuppose knowledge of all the determining knowledge and beliefs of those others who also contribute to its emergence.

Scientism and Constructivism

The corollary of the social theory of complex spontaneous order and of the thoroughly social nature of human reason is Hayek's critique of 'rationalist constructivism', or simply 'constructivism'. This critique has its genesis in his social theory from the 1940s where it first appeared as a critique of what he called 'scientism', or the imitation by the social sciences of the methods of the natural sciences.[87] What, then, is constructivism and why does Hayek reject it as a useful way of understanding complex social processes? He claims that underlying the constructivist view is the presumption that we can, via deliberate action, determine or control the specific outcomes that such processes yield. That is, he claims that constructivism presupposes that

we have it in our power so to shape our institutions that of all possible sets of results that which we prefer to all others will be realized; and that our reason should never resort to automatic or mechanical devices when conscious consideration of all factors would make preferable an outcome different from that of the spontaneous process.[88]

Yet, 'by not recognizing these limits of the powers on individual reason', he writes, it is the constructivists who 'make human reason a less effective instrument than it could be'. Indeed, he adds, 'to act as if we possessed scientific knowledge enabling us to transcend' these limits, 'may itself become a serious obstacle to the advance of the human intellect'.[89]

Yet, despite this critique, and similarly to the conclusion he drew in *The Sensory Order* about our capacity to explain the complex workings of mind, Hayek does *not* want to claim that we are unable to make any useful explanatory or predictive claims about complex social orders. In contrast, to the constructivist view, he claims 'that an effective use of reason requires a proper insight into the limits of the effective use of individual reason in regulating relations between many reasonable beings'.[90] Importantly, we *are* in a position to explain the principles by which such orders emerge and, change and how we can make what he calls non-specific 'pattern predictions' about them.[91] Significantly, it is Charles Darwin's theory of natural selection in biology that he cites here as a prime example of an explanation of a complex phenomenon, although, this is a theory whose underlying logic was first employed, Hayek reminds us, by the social theorists of the Scottish Enlightenment such as David Hume, Adam Smith and Adam Ferguson and only afterwards borrowed by the great theorist of evolution.[92] Moreover, it is not just Darwin's theory of natural selection which fits this mould. Sciences such as astrophysics, the various branches of geophysics (such as seismology, meteorology, geology and oceanography) make use of similar kinds of explanations of the principle by which the phenomena they study operate.[93]

The example of the formation of prices in a market mentioned above is also significant because it illustrates how in Hayek's view it is in economics where the notions of spontaneity and complexity have been most fully grasped. Economic theory, he writes in 'The Theory of Complex Phenomena', 'is confined to describing kinds of patterns which will appear if certain general conditions are satisfied, but can rarely if ever derive from this knowledge any predictions of specific phenomena'. Indeed, just as early theorists of price such as Pareto understood, for Hayek the practical purpose of the theory was not to enable us "'to arrive at a numerical calculation of prices', because it would be 'absurd' to assume that we can ascertain all the data". 'No economist,' he concludes, 'has yet succeeded in making a fortune by buying or selling commodities on the basis of his scientific prediction of future prices (even though some may have done so by selling such predictions)'.[94] Similarly and to attest to his claim about the ubiquity of complex orders in our social life, we would be similarly faced with insuperable difficulties were we to attempt to make detailed predictions of the future linguistic, culinary or sartorial developments of a society.

Despite involving 'mere' explanations of the principle, he claims that 'predictions of a pattern are nevertheless both testable and valuable'and the fact that such explanations do not provide us with the same predictive capacity as do theories of simple phenomena is in Hayek's view irrelevant to their utility.[95] Indeed, and as was the case with our inability to reproduce the calculations of calculating machines, to judge explanations of the principle in these terms would be to judge them by the wrong criteria. In the first instance this relates to the relative certainty of the predictions we can glean from them. Such predictions are relatively less certain than those to be made with respect to simple phenomena only in the sense that they cannot predict *the specific features* of the overall pattern that will emerge. But this is not to say that the more general predictions that they do yield are not themselves certain and capable of confirmation. 'Once we explicitly recognize that the understanding of the general mechanism which produces patterns of a certain kind is not merely a tool for specific predictions but important in its own right, and that it may provide important guides to action (or sometimes indications of the desirability of no action)', he writes, 'we may indeed find that this limited knowledge is most valuable'.[96]

Reason and the cultivation of complex social order

Hayek's claim about our capacity to explain, predict and control the conditions in which spontaneously-emergent complex social order arises is also highly significant for with it he introduces the idea of our deliberately improving or cultivating the institutions that foster it. Indeed, just because the theory of complex phenomena tells us about the conditions in which this order will emerge, it enables us to '*create* such conditions and to observe whether a pattern of the kind predicted will appear', despite our being 'ignorant of many of the particular circumstances' which will determine its particular configuration.[97] The notion of cultivation also allows Hayek to reject what he considers to be the false choice between the centralized determination of the specifics of complex social processes and meekly accepting the outcomes thrown up by them. In the economic sphere, he notes, there is 'all the difference between deliberately creating a system within which competition will work as beneficially as possible and passively accepting institutions as they are'. Indeed, Hayek adds, '[p]robably nothing has done more harm to the liberal cause as the wooden insistence of some liberals on certain rough rules of thumb, above all the principle of laissez faire'.[98] 'The liberal argument', he writes,

> is in favour of making the best possible use of the forces of competition as a means of co-coordinating human effort, not an argument for leaving things just as they are. It is based on the conviction that, where effective competition can be created, it is a better way

of guiding individual efforts than any other. It does not deny, but
even emphasizes, that, in order that competition should work beneficially, *a carefully thought-out legal framework* is required and that
neither the existing nor the past legal rules are free from grave
defects.[99]

The debate about the nature and limits of reason, therefore, is not
a dispute 'on whether we ought to employ foresight and systematic
thinking in planning our common affairs'. Rather, it is 'whether for
this purpose it is better that the holder of coercive power should
confine himself in general to creating conditions under which the
knowledge and initiative of individuals are given the best scope so
that *they* can plan most successfully', or whether this should be done
by central direction according to a predetermined plan.[100] The distinction Hayek wants to draw, then, is not between planning and
chaos. Rather, it is between the use of reason to centrally direct the
specifics of complex social order on the one hand and the use of
reason on the other to consciously cultivate the *circumstances* in which
such order arises. Indeed, his analogy of the deliberate formation of
crystals in a laboratory makes just this point.

> We can never produce crystal or a complex organic compound by
> placing the individual atoms in such a position that they will form
> the lattice of a crystal or the system based on benzol rings which
> make up an organic compound. But we can create the conditions in
> which they will arrange themselves in such a manner.[101]

A hint as to what kind of programme such cultivation and improve-
ment would involve is given in the closing sections of 'Individualism:
True and False' where Hayek first outlines a normative defence of
political individualism. It is an individualism which, 'from the awareness of the limitations of individual knowledge and from the fact that
no person or small group of persons can know all that is known to
somebody', demands 'a strict limitation of all coercive or exclusive
power'.[102] Indeed, it is precisely because human reason is socially constituted that to give power to some to control the social process as
a whole would be to limit that process to the scope of what individual minds can master.[103] More specifically, and given the centrality of
them to his account, Hayek thinks that it is to the kinds of *rules* of just

conduct operative in society that we must pay attention in order to make this cultivation possible.

The Theory of Cultural Evolution

Hayek concedes that the idea of the cultivation of the circumstances conducive to coordination under conditions of social complexity and spontaneous order via the adoption of specific rules presents its own set of difficulties. This is so not least because, as we have seen, many of the rules in question are themselves not the results of conscious design.[104] How, then, do the rules of just conduct themselves come to be adopted and change? Given that our reason only ever develops as a part of a wider social process, Hayek denies the existence of an Archimedean standpoint from which we could judge in any comprehensive fashion all the rules of just conduct that underpin complex spontaneous social order.[105] Consistent with the theory of complex phenomena, the rules, traditions and practices that define the boundaries of permissible action are not determined in advance by any single individual or group. Indeed just as the management of the specifics of the social process in general cannot be passed on to a central authority without fatally compromising its operation, so cannot the process of the selection of its rules.

Again, however, and similar to his claim about the limits of explanation, Hayek does not want to conclude from this insight that we are therefore powerless to judge our rules and traditions. His is no conventionalist but rather claims that we can proceed 'immanently', or from within the system of rules.[106] Thus, for Hayek the process of the selection and alteration of the body of rules is a process of cultural *evolution* rather than conscious human *choice*.[107] Central here is the idea of imitative learning that we saw animated his theory of mind. More specifically, it is via individual migration between norms that the wider body of social rules that shape our actions gradually transforms itself over time.[108] Thus, Hayek concludes, '[t]he structures formed by traditional human practices, are neither natural in the sense of being genetically determined, nor artificial in the sense of being the product of intelligent design, but the result of a process of winnowing or sifting' that occurs through our capacity to imitate what we identify as successful action.[109]

Secondly, and as we shall see in more detail in Chapter 4, the process of selection of rules is also said to be immanent insofar as it occurs via a more formal juridical process in which the acceptability of a rule of just conduct is judged by a person given the authority to do so – and here Hayek has in mind the common law judge – in terms of its consistency, or compatibility, with the wider body of rules of which it is a part when a legal dispute arises.[110] Importantly, Hayek is keen to distance himself from the idea that by invoking the idea of cultural evolution he is drawing any strict analogy with the notion of natural selection in biology. In *The Constitution of Liberty*, for example, he states that 'the decisive factor is not the selection of the physical and inheritable properties of the individuals but the selection by *imitation* of successful institutions and habits'.[111] Hayek, then, is clearly no believer in social Darwinism.[112] The point he is making about cultural evolution is similar to that made by biology with regard to the explanatory power of the theory of natural selection:

> [i]f it were possible to ascertain the particular facts of the past which operated on the selection of the particular forms that emerged, it would provide a complete explanation of the structure of the existing organisms; and similarly, if it were possible to ascertain all the particular facts which will operate on them during some future period, it ought to enable us to predict future development. But, of course, we will never be able to do either, because science has no means of ascertaining all the particular facts that it would have to possess to perform such a feat.[113]

Indeed, Hayek explicitly states that he does not wish to claim that the criterion of selection is either 'survival of the fittest', 'the struggle for existence' or natural selection in the biological sense.[114] It seems, therefore, that the relevant criterion is the persistence of cultural groups and of the individuals that comprise them, although this has attracted criticism from some commentators.[115]

We have seen that Hayek offers a complex and challenging theory of mind and society, the central aspect of which is the Knowledge Problem and its implications for our understanding and mastery of complex social processes. What, though, are the practical and normative implications of Hayek's social theory? It is to answering this question that we turn next, as we see how Hayek's epistemological research programme informed his initial interest in one particular aspect of the spontaneous order of a complex society: its economy.

Notes

[1] Hayek, F. A., *The Sensory Order: An Inquiry into the Foundations of Theoretical Psychology*, London, Routledge and Kegan Paul, 1952a; Hayek, F. A., 'Rules, Perception and Intelligibility', in Hayek, F. A. (ed.), *Studies in Philosophy, Politics and Economics*, London, Routledge and Kegan Paul, (1962a) 1967, pp. 43–65; Hayek, F. A., 'The Primacy of the Abstract', in Hayek, F. A. (ed.), *New Studies in Philosophy, Politics, Economics and the History of Ideas*, London Routledge and Kegan Paul, (1969) 1978, pp. 35–49. Hayek's theory is similar – although, to be sure, independently arrived-at – to that of psychologist Donald Hebb. On this see *The Sensory Order*, §2.49, footnote 1; Hebb, D. O., *The Organization of Behavior*, Mahwah, NJ, Laurence Erlbaum, (1949) 2002. It has also been shown to prefigure in several important respects later work in cognitive science, artificial intelligence, neural network modelling, cybernetics, systems theory and neuropsychology. See Edelman, G., 'Through a Computer Darkly: Group Selection and Higher Brain Function', *Bulletin of the American Academy of Arts and Sciences*, vol. 36, no. 1, 1982, pp. 20–49; Fuster, J., *Memory in the Cerebral Cortex: An Empirical Approach to Neural networks in the Human and Nonhuman Primate*, Cambridge, MIT Press, 1995; 'Network Memory', *Trends in Neurosciences,* vol. 20, no. 10, 1997, pp. 451–459; Pinker, S., *The Blank Slate: The Modern Denial of Human Nature*, London, Penguin, 2003, p. 292; Rosenblatt, F., 'The Perceptron: a Probabilistic Model for Information Storage and Organization in the Brain, *Psychological Review*, vol. 65, 1958, pp. 386–408. On the Artificial Intelligence implications of Hayek's theory see *The Sensory Order*, §§ 8.81–8.82.

[2] See Hayek, F. A., *The Political Order of a Free People*, London, Routledge, 1979, pp. 199–200, n. 26.

[3] Hayek, *The Sensory Order,* §§1.6–1.21.

[4] Ibid., §1.13.

[5] Ibid., §§1.18. See also Ibid., §1.21.

[6] Ibid., §§3.1–3.14.

[7] Ibid., §8.3.

[8] Ibid., §5.11.

[9] Ibid., §2.49.

[10] Ibid., §§1.31–1.37. See also Ibid., §3.5; Hayek, 'The Primacy of the Abstract', pp. 36–37.

[11] Hayek, *The Sensory Order,* §§ 2.49. See also Ibid., §1.35.

[12] Ibid., §2.50, emphasis added.

[13] Klüver, H., 'Introduction', in Hayek, *The Sensory Order*, p. xviii.

[14] Ibid.

[15] Hayek, op. cit., §§5.2–5.4, emphasis added. Kant, I., *The Critique of Pure Reason*, Cambridge, Cambridge University Press, (1781/1787) 1998.

[16] Ayer, A. J., *The Problem of Knowledge*, London, MacMillan, 1956, chapter 5; Mill, J. S., *An Examination of Sir William Hamilton's Philosophy*, London, Longmans, Green and Company, (1865) 1889, chapter 12; Russell, B., 'Analogy', in Russell, B. (ed.), *Human Knowledge: Its Scope and Limits*, Abingdon, Routledge (1948) 2009, pp. 425–428.

17 Hayek, op. cit.,§1.68.
18 Hayek, 'Rules, Perception and Intelligibility', p. 56.
19 Hayek, 'The Primacy of the Abstract', pp. 39–42.
20 Ibid., pp. 45–48.
21 Ibid., pp. 37–42, 43–47, 55–60.
22 Hayek, 'Rules, Percpetion and Intelligibility', p. 47.
23 Hayek, *The Sensory Order*, §1.69. Hayek also appeals to experimental methods in this regard. See Ibid., §1.71.
24 Hayek, 'Rules, Perception and Intelligibility', pp. 43–45; 'The Primacy of the Abstract', pp. 39–40.
25 Hayek, 'Rules, Perception and Intelligibility', pp. 47–48, 54–55; 'The Primacy of the Abstract', p. 38.
26 Ibid., §§5.17–5.49.
27 Ibid., §§5.42–5.43.
28 Ibid., §§6.29–6.52.
29 Ibid., §5.41.
30 Ibid., §8.14.
31 Ibid., §5.27.
32 Ibid., §8.66.
33 Ibid., §8.69 .
34 Ibid., §8.87. See also, §8.46–8.47.
35 Ibid., §8.92.
36 Ibid., §§2.18–2.19. See also, 5.77–5.91.
37 Ibid., §8.94.
38 Hayek, F. A., *The Counter-Revolution of Science: Studies in the Abuse of Reason*, Indianapolis, Liberty Press, 1952b, pp. 60. See also, p. 40.
39 Hayek, *The Sensory Order*, §8.93.
40 Hayek, *The Counter-Revolution of Science*, p. 37.
41 Ibid., p. 57, emphasis added. See also Hayek, F. A., 'The Facts of the Social Sciences', in Hayek, F. A. (ed.), *Individualism and Economic Order*, Chicago, IL, University of Chicago Press, (1942) 1948, pp. 57–76; Hayek, F. A., 'Individualism: True and False', in Hayek, F. A. (ed.), *Individualism and Economic Order*, Chicago, IL, University of Chicago Press, (1946a) 1948, pp. 1–32.
42 Hayek, 'The Facts of the Social Sciences', p. 60, emphasis added. See also Hayek, *The Counter-Revolution of Science*, pp. 44–53, 57–58 and *The Sensory Order*, §§ 1.90–1.107.
43 Hayek, *The Counter-Revolution of Science*, p. 47.
44 Hayek, 'The Facts of the Social Sciences', p. 62.
45 Hayek, *The Counter-Revolution of Science*, pp. 43–44.
46 Ibid., p. 47.
47 Ibid. See also Hayek, 'The Facts of the Social Sciences', pp. 60–64.
48 Ibid., p. 48.
49 Hayek, 'The Facts of the Social Sciences', p. 66. See also Hayek, *The Counter-Revolution of Science*, pp. 134–136 and 'Rules, Perception and Intelligibility', pp. 46, 60.
50 For an overview see Crossley, *Intersubjectivity: The Fabric of Social Becoming*, London, Sage Publications, 1996.

[51] Hayek, *The Counter-Revolution of Science*, p. 40. See also, p. 69 and Hyek, *The Sensory Order*, §§ 8.87–8.98.

[52] Ibid., p. 39, emphasis added.

[53] Hayek does not actually cite this natural world example but see, Hayek, *The Political Ideal of the Rule of Law*, Cairo, National Bank of Egypt, 1955a, pp. 30–31; Hayek, F. A., *Rules and Order*, London, Routledge, 1973, pp. 39–40.

[54] Bonar quoted in Hayek, 'Individualism: True and False', p. 10, n. 14. See also Hayek, *The Counter-Revolution of Science*, pp. 70–71.

[55] See, Hayek, *The Counter-Revolution of Science*, pp. 68–69; 'The Facts of the Social Sciences', p. 72; *Rules and Order*, p. 38.

[56] Hayek, F. A., 'The Results of Human Action but not of Human Design', in Hayek, F. A. (ed.), *Studies in Philosophy, Politics and Economics*, London, Routledge and Kegan Paul, 1967b, pp. 96.

[57] Hayek, 'The Facts of the Social Sciences', p. 76.

[58] See Hayek, F. A., 'The Nature and History of the Problem', in Hayek, F. A. (ed.), *Collectivist Economic Planning: Critical Studies on The Possibilities Of Socialism*, Auburn, AL, The Ludwig von Mises Institute, (1935) 2009, p. 10. See also Hayek, F. A., 'Degrees of Explanation', in Hayek, F. A. (ed.), *Studies in Philosophy, Politics and Economics*, London, Routledge and Kegan Paul, (1955b) 1967, pp. 3–21; Hayek, F. A., 'The Theory of Complex Phenomena', in Hayek, F. A. (ed.), *Studies in Philosophy, Politics and Economics*, London, Routledge and Kegan Paul, (1964a) 1967, pp. 22–42.

[59] *Rules and Order*, p. 38. See also Hayek, F.A., 'The Confusion of Language in Political Thought', in Hayek, F. A., *New Studies in Philosophy, Politics, Economics and the History of Ideas*, London, Routledge and Kegan Paul, (1968a) 1978, pp. 72–6

[60] Hayek, *The Counter-Revolution of Science*, p. 49.

[61] Ibid., p. 50.

[62] Ibid., pp. 149–150. See also, pp. 145–146, 153–164.

[63] See Hayek, 'Notes on the Evolution of Systems of Rules of Conduct', in Hayek, F.A. (ed.), *Studies in Philosophy, Politics and Economics*, London, Routledge and Kegan Paul, 1967a, p. 67; Hayek, *Rules and Order*, pp. 17–19, 75.

[64] Hayek, *The Political Ideal of the Rule of Law*, pp. 30–31. See also Hayek, F. A., *The Constitution of Liberty*, London, Routledge, 1960, pp. 54–70; Hayek, F. A., 'Kinds of Rationalism', in Hayek, F. A. (ed.), *Studies in Philosophy, Politics and Economics*, London, Routledge and Kegan Paul, (1965) 1967, pp. 82–95; Hayek, F. A., 'Notes on the Evolution of Systems of Rules of Conduct', in Hayek, F. A. (ed.), *Studies in Philosophy, Politics and Economics*, London, Routledge and Kegan Paul, 1967a, pp. 66–81; Hayek, F. A., 'The Results of Human Action but not of Human Design', pp. 96–105; Hayek, F. A., 'The Errors of Constructivism', in Hayek, F. A. (ed.), *New Studies in Philosophy, Politics, Economics and the History of Ideas*, London, Routledge and Kegan Paul, (1970) 1978, pp. 3–22; Hayek, *Rules and Order*, pp. 17–19, 45.

[65] Hayek, *Rules and Order*, p. 13. See also Hayek, *The Political Ideal of the Rule of Law*, pp. 29–31; 'Kinds of Rationalism', pp. 90–91.

[66] See Hayek, 'Rules, Perception and Intelligibility', p. 56; 'The Errors of Constructivism', p. 10; Hayek, F. A., *The Mirage of Social Justice*, London, Routledge, 1976a, p. 11.

[67] Hayek, 'Notes on the Evolution of Systems of Rules of Conduct', p. 81. See also Hayek, 'Rules, Perception and Intelligibility', pp. 56–57; 'The Errors of Constructivism', pp. 7–8.

[68] See Hayek, *The Constitution of Liberty*, pp. 24–25, 27–28; 'The Errors of Constructivism', p. 10; *Rules and Order*, pp. 11–12; *The Mirage of Social Justice*, p. 4.

[69] Hayek, F. A., *Knowledge, Evolution and Society*, London, Adam Smith Institute, 1983, pp. 45–46.

[70] Hayek, *The Constitution of Liberty*, p. 27. See also, pp. 24–25; *The Counter-Revolution of Science*, pp. 149–150.

[71] Ibid., pp. 28–29. See also Hayek, *Rules and Order*, pp. 72–78.

[72] See Hayek, 'The Errors of Constructivism', p. 9; 'Notes on the Evolution of Systems of Rules of Conduct', p. 67; *Rules and Order*, pp. 43–44.

[73] Hayek, *Rules and Order*, p. 50. See also Hayek, *The Constitution of Liberty*, pp. 148–161.

[74] Hayek, *The Road to Serfdom*, p. 74.

[75] Hayek, *Rules and Order*, p. 51.

[76] Ibid., p. 43.

[77] SeeIbid., pp. 36–38, 46–54; Hayek, 'The Confusion of Language in Political Thought', pp. 72–76.

[78] Hayek, *Rules and Order*, p. 49.

[79] Ibid., p. 47.

[80] Ibid., pp. 15–16. See also Hayek, *The Political Ideal of the Rule of Law*, pp. 30–31; 'Kinds of Rationalism', pp. 92–93.

[81] Hayek, 'Degrees of Explanation', p. 15. See also Hayek, 'The Theory of Complex Phenomena', p. 34; 'The Errors of Constructivism', p. 12; 'The Pretence of Knowledge', pp. 24, 26.

[82] Hayek, 'Individualism: True and False', p. 6. See also, *The Counter-Revolution of Science*, pp. 151–152.

[83] Hayek, *The Counter-Revolution of Science*, pp. 145–146.

[84] Hayek, 'Individualism: True and False', p. 6. On comunitarianism see MacIntyre, A., *Whose Justice? Which Rationality?*, Notre Dame, Notre Dame University Press, 1988; Sandel, M., *Liberalism and the Limits of Justice*, Cambridge, Cambridge University Press, 1982; Taylor, C., *Sources of the Self*, Harvard, Harvard University Press, 1989; Walzer, M., *Spheres of Justice*, New York, Basic Books, 1983. For an overview see Mulhall, S. and Swift, A., *Liberals and Communitarians*, 2nd ed., Oxford, Blackwell, 1996; Butler, J., *Giving an Account of Oneself*, New York, Fordham University Press, 2005.

[85] Ibid., p. 15.

[86] Hayek, *Rules and Order*, p. 17. See also Hayek, *The Counter-Revolution of Science*, p. 160; *The Constitution of Liberty*, p. 24.

[87] Hayek, *The Counter-Revolution of Science*, pp. 76–182. For the important criticisms of Hayek's earlier views on the differences between the natural and social sciences see Nagel, E., '[Review of] Hayek, *The Counter-Revolution of*

Science', *Journal of Philosophy*, vol. 49, no. 17, (August) 1952, pp. 560–565; Popper, K., *The Open Society and Its Enemies*, vol. I, London, Routledge and Kegan Paul, 1945, pp. 285–286, n. 4; *The Poverty of Historicism*, London, Routledge, (1944/1945, 1957) 2002, pp. 126–132; Watkins, J. W. N., '[Review of] Hayek, *The Counter-Revolution of Science*', *Ethics*, vol. 64, no. 1, 1953, pp. 56–59. See also Uebel, T. E., 'Some Scientism, Some Historicism, Some Critics,' in Stone, M. W. F. and Wolff, J. (eds), *The Proper Ambition of Science*, London, Routledge, 2000, pp. 151–173.

88 Hayek, 'Kinds of Rationalism', p. 85. See also Hayek, 'The Errors of Constructivism', p. 6; *Rules and Order*, chapter 1.

89 Hayek, 'The Pretence of Knowledge', p. 32. See also Hayek, *The Counter-Revolution of Science*, p. 158; 'Individualism: True and False', p. 33; 'Degrees of Explanation', p. 16.

90 Hayek, 'Kinds of Rationalism', p. 84.

91 Hayek, 'The Theory of Complex Phenomena', pp. 22–34

92 See Hayek, F. A., 'The Legal and Political Philosophy of David Hume', in Hayek, F. A. (ed.), *Studies in Philosophy, Politics and Economics*, London, Routledge and Kegan Paul, (1964b) 1967, pp. 111, 119; 'The Results of Human Action but not of Human Design', p. 103, n. 21; Hayek, F. A., 'Dr. Bernard Mandeville', in Hayek, F. A. (ed.), *New Studies in Philosophy, Politics, Economics and the History of Ideas*, London, Routledge and Kegan Paul, (1967d) 1978, p. 265; 'The Errors of Constructivism', p.9; *Rules and Order*, pp. 16, 22–23; Hayek, F. A., 'The Atavism of Social Justice', in Hayek, F. A. (ed.), *New Studies in Philosophy, Politics, Economic and the History of Ideas*, London, Routledge and Kegan Paul, (1976c) 1978, p. 68; *The Political Order of a Free People*, p. 154.

93 See Hayek, 'Degrees of Explanation', pp. 3–4, 20–21; 'The Theory of Complex Phenomena', pp. 24–27, 31–36; Hayek, F. A., 'Competition as a Discovery Procedure', *The Quarterly Journal of Austrian Economics*, vol. 5, no. 3, (1968b) 2002, pp. 9–23, p. 11; *Rules and Order*, pp. 15–17.

94 Hayek, 'The Theory of Complex Phenomena', p. 35. Hayek's quotation is from Pareto, V., *Manuel d'économie politique*, 2nd ed., Paris, 1927, pp. 223–224. See also Hayek, 'The Pretence of Knowledge', pp. 32–33.

95 Ibid., pp. 36, 28.

96 Ibid., p. 40. See also Hayek, 'Degrees of Explanation', pp. 16–17.

97 Ibid., p. 36, emphasis added. See also Hayek, *The Counter-Revolution of Science*, pp. 160–161; 'Degrees of Explanation', p. 18.

98 Hayek, *The Road to Serfdom*, p. 17.

99 Ibid., p. 36, emphasis added.

100 Ibid., p. 35.

101 Hayek, *Rules and Order*, pp. 39–40.

102 Hayek, 'Individualism: True and False', p. 16.

103 Ibid., p. 32. See also Hayek, *The Counter-Revolution of Science*, p. 158.

104 Hayek, 'Kinds of Rationalism', p. 92.

105 Hayek, 'The Errors of Constructivism', p. 20.

106 Ibid., p. 7.

107 Hayek, 'Notes on the Evolution of Systems of Rules of Conduct', p. 67; 'The Errors of Constructivism', pp.7, 9–10; *Rules and Order*, pp. 18–19; *The Political Order of a Free People*, pp. 155–156.

108 Hayek, 'Nature v. Nurture Once Again', *New Studies in Philosophy, Politics, Economics and the History of Ideas*, London, Routledge and Kegan Paul, (1971) 1978, p. 292.

109 Hayek, *The Political Order of a Free People*, p. 155.

110 Hayek, 'The Errors of Constructivism', p. 19.

111 Hayek, The *Constitution of Liberty*, p. 59, emphasis added. See also Hayek, F. A., 'Nature v. Nurture Once Again', p. 291; 'The Errors of Constructivism', p. 7; *The Political Order of a Free People*, p. 159.

112 Hayek, *Rules and Order*, p. 23.

113 Ibid., p. 16.

114 Hayek, *The Constitution of Liberty*, p. 59.

115 See Hayek, *Rules and Order*, pp. 18–19; *The Political Order of a Free People*, pp. 155–159; 'The Errors of Constructivism', pp. 19–20; 'Kinds of Rationalism', p. 86; 'Notes on the Evolution of Systems of Rules of Conduct', p. 69. For a critical assessment of Hayek's view of cultural evolution see Vanberg, V., 'Spontaneous Market Order and Social Rules: A Critical Examination of F. A. Hayek's Theory of Cultural Evolution', *Economics and Philosophy*, vol. 2, April 1986, pp. 75–100.

3

Economics, the State and Social Justice

Economic Theory and Practice

The Knowledge Problem and the idea of general equilibrium

In the last chapter we saw how Hayek's social theory has its logical roots in his theory of mind and seeks to explain the operation of complex societies. In this work he not only stresses the idea of the proper specification of the power of our reason with respect to our capacity to plan the detail of spontaneously-emergent complex social order but also to derive a *normative* thesis about our proper organizational stance towards social complexity, given the existence of the Knowledge Problem. This chapter focuses in more detail on these two themes by looking at one of Hayek's most well-known applications of the Knowledge Problem: its relationship to economic theory and practice. More specifically, we will investigate Hayek's views on reason and social organization by looking at four aspects of his contribution to economics: 1) his qualified scepticism about the usefulness of the concept of general equilibrium as a tool for explaining the workings of the market economy, 2) his contribution to the socialist calculation debate about the possibility of centralized economic planning, 3) his conception of the free market as a knowledge coordinating 'discovery procedure' and 4) his views on distributive or 'social' justice in which the state takes an active role in correcting the outcomes of the market.

As with so much of his thought, Hayek's views on general equilibrium are derived from his epistemologically grounded social theory and the Knowledge Problem that is at its core. Just as we saw that the knowledge relevant to the formation of complex social order in general is only ever dispersed, fleeting and of a practical nature, 'the peculiar character of the problem of a rational economic order', Hayek writes in 'The Use of Knowledge in Society', 'is determined precisely by the fact that the knowledge of the circumstances of which we must make use never exists in concentrated or integrated form, but solely as the dispersed bits of incomplete and frequently contradictory knowledge which all the separate individuals possess'.[1] How, though, does the Knowledge Problem relate to the notion of general equilibrium?

The notion of general equilibrium, pioneered in the work of neoclassical economists such as Léon Walras, is a theoretical model by which the general properties of markets may be clarified and understood.[2] More specifically, it is a full information model of economic coordination that presupposes that all economic agents have access to the same objectively correct information – captured in the expression 'full data'. This assumption is crucial because it means that economic actors are therefore in a position to coordinate their plans so that supply meets demand and all available goods on the market sell, or 'clear'.[3] Scepticism about whether a state of equilibrium ever actually exists in any particular market sector or indeed, in the market, as a whole, was central to Hayek's economic thought. The difficulty he identifies here is that the notion of a market being in equilibrium turns economics into a branch of pure logic, Hayek calls it 'the Pure Logic of Choice', or 'a set of self-evident propositions which, like mathematics or geometry, are subject to no other test but internal consistency'.[4] As he claims in 'Economics and Knowledge', in this conception 'all the members of the community, even if they are not supposed to be strictly omniscient, are at least supposed to know automatically all that is relevant for their decisions' to co-ordinate with those of their fellows.[5]

Yet precisely because of this strong knowledge assumption, Hayek contends that economics as a discipline has exaggerated the usefulness of the general equilibrium construct in two respects. First, he questions its usefulness as a device for deriving empirically verifiable explanations and predictions about the specifics of the economic process. Secondly, Hayek questions general equilibrium theory's capacity to serve as the theoretical basis for deriving useful evaluative statements about the advantages and disadvantages of different types of economic system such as those made about capitalism, socialism or communism. In both cases, Hayek argues that the extension of the general equilibrium construct to these areas is problematic because it provides no answer to the question of how knowledge is actually communicated across the economy of a complex society, but rather assumes that this has already taken place. That is, because general equilibrium theory 'in effect starts from the assumption that people's *knowledge* corresponds with the objective *facts* of the situation', 'it systematically leaves out what is our main task to explain' because such correspondence would presuppose the possibility of centralizing that knowledge.[6] Thus, because the general equilibrium model assumes full data or given knowledge, that is, because it is based upon the assumption that knowledge coordination has already occurred, it only obscures the process by which real markets deal with the Knowledge Problem.[7] The Knowledge Problem, Hayek claims, is

> in no way solved if we can show that all the facts, *if* they are known to a single mind, would uniquely determine the solution; instead we must show how a solution is produced by interactions of people each of whom possess only partial knowledge. To assume all the knowledge to be given to a single mind...is to assume the problem away and to disregard everything that is important and significant in the real world.[8]

This situation that general equilibrium represents was described by Hayek's mentor Mises as that of 'the evenly rotating economy' in which the decision-making needed to adapt to ever-changing circumstances is no longer necessary.[9] Hayek, too, encapsulated its logic in the paper 'The Meaning of Competition' where he claims that 'if no such adaptations were required, if at any moment we knew that all change had stopped and things would forever go on exactly as they are now, there would be no more questions of the use of resources to be solved'.[10] At a more general level, the idea of the evenly rotating economy also has its social correlate in Mises' notion of the 'stationary society', as well as in writer Yevgeny Zamyatin's description, in his 1921 dystopian novel *We*, of the ideal of a society as one that is 'in a condition where nothing *happens* any more'.[11]

In contrast to the mainstream view, and with his radically different assumption about the status of the knowledge relevant to economic decision-making, the task of economic theory for Hayek is shifted away from the attempt to describe an end-state of equilibrium towards a procedural explanation of how it is possible that 'the combination of fragments of knowledge existing in different minds bring[s] about results which, if they were to be brought about deliberately, would require a knowledge on the part of the directing mind which no single person can possess'.[12] Hayek thus shifts theoretical attention away from explaining a state of affairs that presupposes that the knowledge relevant to our decisions in the market is already coordinated, towards an explanation of the *process* of how it is actually communicated to us in the absence of it ever being given *in toto* to anybody. Economic theory, therefore, must not just define an end state. It also needs to explain how the market process actually works, or of how the knowledge, or what Hayek calls the '"data" of the different individuals on which they base their plans are adjusted to the objective facts of their environment (which includes the actions of other people)'.[13]

To be sure, Hayek does not wish to deny that the notion of general equilibrium is both useful and fruitful.[14] Its assumption concerning given or perfect knowledge is, for example, useful insofar as it clarifies how, if there were an observable tendency for markets to be in equilibrium, this would mean that we could with confidence claim that the knowledge of mutually ignorant individuals was being coordinated. However, as he was keen to point out on numerous occasions, the pioneers of general equilibrium theory such as Walras and Pareto never meant for its assumptions to be true of any real world state of affairs. Indeed, Pareto himself clearly thought it 'absurd' to assume that we could know all that we would need to know about objective economic conditions in order to make correct predictions of specific prices.[15] General equilibrium's usefulness must only ever be a limited one in the absence of an account of how social knowledge 'is acquired and communicated'.[16]

The qualified scepticism with which Hayek treats what he considers to be the epistemological pretensions of general equilibrium theory is also significant for his views on the practicalities of economic organization. More specifically, it is a scepticism that can be seen to colour his critique, written at around this time, of what he initially called scientism and which, as we saw in the last chapter, eventually became his argument against constructivism. Thus, in papers such as 'Freedom and the Economic System' and, more extensively, in *The Road to Serfdom*, Hayek claims that scientism's underlying epistemological commitments have made possible many of the political stances he wants to reject.[17] Also written during the 1940's, along with the writings on scientism to be found in the paper 'Individualism: True and False' and the essays that were published as *The Counter-Revolution of Science*, *The Road to Serfdom* was intended as the final part of a project about the nature and genesis of scientism, and the practical consequences of its adoption.[18] This book is also significant because it speaks directly to the central issue of how we determine the of the proper role of that organization whose aim is to guarantee the integrity of the rules of just conduct: the state. Citing the then contemporary examples of Soviet Russia and Nazi Germany, Hayek claims that the adoption of central planning by the state that acceptance of the tenets of 'scientism' and 'false individualism' makes possible inevitably leads to the destruction of individual freedom itself. This is so not least because practical necessity soon demands the installation of people in positions of executive authority prepared to take and enforce tough decisions when centrally determined plans begin to fail. Significantly, then, Hayek links the question of the *rationality* of central planning to its effects upon individual *liberty*, arguing that a centrally planned economy inevitably leads to a totalitarian state. In order to get a clearer idea of how these two ideas gel in Hayek's mind we need, therefore, to examine his critique of central planning.

The socialist calculation debate

Hayek's contribution builds upon and extends that of Mises, who is most commonly credited with having offered the first epistemological critique of central planning. In a 1920 article, 'Economic Calculation in the Socialist Commonwealth', and later in more extensive form in his *Socialism: An Economic and Sociological Analysis*, Mises argued that a price system was essential for rational economic calculation. Central to his argument is the claim that prices are not only conveyors of information concerning the availability of resources. They also allow for cost comparison between the different kinds of resources and production processes that could be employed to produce the same good and therefore help to ensure that resources are devoted to their most productive use. Importantly, the idea of the means of production being privately owned was also crucial to Mises' argument because the only way in which prices for resources could emerge would be for it to be legally possible to buy and sell them. We can clarify Mises' argument by looking at the problem of knowing whether resource x or resource y should be employed to produce consumer good G. When a change in local conditions reduces the availability of x in an economy with a price mechanism, this is accompanied by an increase in its price. In response to this producers of G, who use x in their production process, have two options. Firstly, they can simply raise the price of G so as to make up for the shortfall in earnings brought about by the increase in

their production costs. Alternatively, they can switch from *x* to resource
y which, whilst formerly more expensive, is now cheaper than *x*. In the
first case the final price of G which consumers pay will be significantly
higher than before, whilst in the second it will still be higher, but less so
than in the first case. Seeking to protect their market share, producers
of G therefore switch from *x* to *y*, and G's raised price is passed along
the production chain from the resource extraction sites, to the factories,
the wholesalers, and finally to consumers. Most importantly for Mises'
epistemological argument, and without any knowledge of local conditions in distant *x*- and *y*-producing regions, consumers not only end up
consuming less of *x* and more of *y* in their G, but less of G in general,
"as if" they had been ordered to do so, when in fact no such order was
ever given. By contrast, if the means of production were not privately
owned – as they would not be in a centrally planned economy – it would
be extraordinarily difficult to establish prices for *x* and *y* that reflected
changes in their relative cost.[19] The absence of prices, then, presented
socialism with a serious problem because without them there would
be no way of determining the best use of resources.[20] Mises therefore
concluded that central planning would ultimately fail because, without
a price system, the amount of information relevant to deciding upon
the best use of resources would be too great to handle.

Of course, Mises' argument did not go unanswered. Whilst accepting its force and particularly the need for prices even in a socialist
economy, Hayek's colleague at the LSE, Oscar Lange, denied that
Mises' critique dealt a fatal blow to socialism. In response he proposed
a method of generating prices by central planning boards through
trial and error, where upward or downward price adjustments for the
various factors of production would be made incrementally as changes
occurred in their relative scarcity and availability. Information about
shortages or surpluses would thus be conveyed to the central planning
board by the managers of state-owned firms and with the consequent
adjustments made based on this information, the problem presented
by the absence of prices would be overcome.

This 'Lange Model' was one of the earliest examples of market
socialism and it was against it that Hayek argued in a series of papers
throughout the late 1930s and 1940s. Importantly, central to Hayek's
response to Lange was more than the empirical claim that Mises made
concerning the practical difficulty of conscious coordination of complex economic processes from the centre. Rather, he argued that the
Knowledge Problem would make such coordination *impossible*.[21] Thus,

from the Misesian assumption that the dispersed knowledge required for economic calculation in the socialist commonwealth is, albeit with significant difficulty, available, Hayekian economic theory moves to the assumption that, in principle, it is not. Hayek strengthens the argument is this way by investigating the presuppositions lying behind neoclassical general equilibrium theory, for it is these that, erroneously in his view, make at least theoretically possible the kind of market-socialist model Lange defends. Thus, whilst 'Economics and Knowledge' is primarily a paper about the usefulness of the concept of equilibrium to economic theory, Hayek also believed that his reformulation of the economic problem faced by a complex society had important consequences for economic policy. Indeed he claims that

> [o]ne of the chief results of the theory of the market economy is thus that in certain conditions...competition produces an adaptation to countless circumstances which in their totality are not known and cannot be known to any person or authority, and that therefore this adaptation cannot be brought about by a central direction of all economic activity.[22]

Hayek's views on the practical implications of the Knowledge Problem are also given detailed treatment in another important paper from this period, 'The Use of Knowledge in Society'. Here he considers what problem would need to be solved in order to create and maintain what he called a 'rational economic order'; that is, an economic order whose specific outcomes are brought about via central planning.[23] Unlike the economic problems faced by engineers who have to decide which combinations of resources to expend in achieving their predetermined projects, the economic Knowledge Problem faced by society as a whole is of an entirely different nature: it is a problem of the utilization of resources where it is not clear to which ends they should be employed.[24] Now '[o]n certain familiar assumptions', Hayek writes, the answer to this problem 'is simple enough'.

> *If* we possess all the relevant information, *if* we can start out from a given system of preferences and *if* we command complete knowledge of available means, the problem which remains is purely one of logic. That is the answer to the question of what is the best use of available means is implicit in our assumptions.[25]

However, as was the case with his theoretical analysis of the general equilibrium construct, for Hayek these assumptions do not hold because 'the "data" from which the economic calculus starts are never given to a single mind which could work out the implications and can never be so given'.[26] Precisely because of the existence of the Knowledge Problem neither individual citizens, nor state actors, would ever be privy to all the information necessary for rational economic calculation in a complex society. It is for this reason that, as several commentators have made clear, for Hayek the problem faced by central planners is not only a calculational problem where they simply need to decide where to allocate resources on the basis of given knowledge but which, in the absence of prices, they cannot do. It is an *epistemological* one where an adequate account of how dispersed, fleeting and tacitly held social knowledge is actually communicated in a complex economic order must first be given. Just as with the exaggeration of the theoretical utility of the notion of general equilibrium, without such an account all that is achieved is an assumption of the conditions which the market is supposed to cope with.[27] The problem of coordination under conditions of economic complexity returns us to the role of private property rights and prices introduced by Mises. For Hayek, it is the price mechanism of the market that serves this knowledge coordinating role necessary to the explanation that he claims Lange's model cannot give. It is to his account of the market order, then, that we now turn.

The Free Market as an Economic Discovery Procedure

Economy and catallaxy

Even if we accept Hayek's critique of the theoretical applicability of general equilibrium theory's core assumptions and of the practical usefulness of applying them in debates about real-world institutions, we still need an account of how we should understand markets and of how we should judge their results. These were questions which Hayek began to answer as early as the 1940s in papers such as 'The Meaning of Competition', but it was only in the later stages of his career that his conception reached full fruition as a theory of the market order. The answers that Hayek gives to these questions are that (a) we should understand the market economy as a 'catallactic' discovery procedure and (b) that, precisely because of the existence of the Knowledge Problem to which markets respond, their results cannot properly be judged in absolute or objective terms but only *relative to other kinds of institutional arrangement.*

The idea of the free market as a discovery procedure is intimately related to its underlying rationale, and emerges from a distinction Hayek makes between the economy and what he calls the *catallaxy*.[28] In common usage, by the 'economy' we usually mean the national economy of a country. Somewhat confusingly, however, we also describe the small-scale entities such as firms, farms or family units as having 'economies'. Yet, for Hayek, doing so obscures a crucial difference between the two kinds of economy. In the case of a firm or household economy, the ends around which decisions are made are generally known in advance and decisions about resource allocation are therefore relatively uncomplicated. In this sense, then, for Hayek a household economy, like that of a firm or a farm, is the economy of an organization, *or taxis*. However, the same does not hold in Hayek's view for the economy of a large-scale complex society. Owing to its size and the indirect nature of the social relationships within it, Hayek contends that the Knowledge Problem that the economy of such a society consequently faces means that it is not immediately apparent to what use resources should be put. For this reason, then, Hayek employs the term '*catallaxy*' to describe the economic aspect of the complex spontaneous order, or *cosmos*, of a large-scale society.

The distinction between an economy and a *catallaxy* is important because the epistemological circumstances that mark the latter also point to the rationale for the competitive process that occurs within it. Here Hayek draws an analogy with the playing of games where a competition is instituted precisely because the outcome is unknown. 'In sporting events, examinations, the awarding of government contracts, or the bestowal of prizes for poems, not to mention science', he writes in 'Competition as a Discovery Procedure', 'it would be patently absurd to sponsor a contest if we knew who the winner would be'.[29] Similarly, for Hayek, competition is useful in complex societies precisely because we cannot know what the appropriate specific outcome should be, given that we cannot have direct access to all the knowledge of the circumstances relevant to determining it. By contrast, competition would not make much sense within a household economy precisely because it *is* broadly known in advance how economic questions ought to be determined. Notable in Hayek's account of *catallaxy*, moreover, is the absence of an *ethical* rationale for competition where it is considered as important because it is the economic manifestation of our having a natural right to property, as in the case of Locke.[30] Rather it is upon the *epistemological* exigencies of the Knowledge Problem that, for Hayek, these economic rights are properly founded.

Catallactic optima and the evaluation of market outcomes

According to Hayek, the epistemological rationale for the market also has important consequences for the manner in which we judge its results. Surprisingly, however, because it is a method for the discovery of what should be done with resources in the face of the Knowledge Problem, he claims that competition can never actually be *proven* in absolute terms to be the best method for doing. In order, for example, to see competition's usefulness in any objective sense, we would first have to have a clear idea of the relevant optimal allocation. With knowledge of this optimum we would then have an appropriate comparative yardstick to see how close the market process, or some alternative to it, came to success. Of course, for Hayek, such an optimum in virtue of which we could assess competition's efficacy is precisely what we are seeking to discover via competition. If 'we do not know in advance the facts we wish to discover with the help of competition', he explains, 'we are also unable to determine how effectively competition leads to the discovery of all the relevant circumstances that could have been discovered'.[31] Thus, we cannot recommend the market because it will deliver us an identifiable specific allocation of resources. That would be to presuppose, in a manner identical to the presuppositions of general equilibrium theory, knowledge of the optimum we seek to discover. By the same token, however, the unique epistemological rationale for competition that Hayek gives also means that we should not say that competition is an *inadequate* means of determining allocational questions just because it cannot ensure that a specific 'perfect' distribution will be brought about. The point that Hayek seeks to make, then, is that, given dispersed, fleeting and tacit knowledge, we do not know which distribution is optimal, because knowing that would be dependent upon knowledge of circumstances that is never given to us in their entirety.

Hayek also makes this important point about the proper evaluative stance with respect market outcomes by analogy with scientific method. It would not make much sense, he claims, to ask how effective science was at discovering facts about of the natural world in absolute terms because this is precisely what it is tasked to do. Similar to the market, scientific method cannot be tested for its efficacy relative to an objective standard, for doing so would only make sense if our knowledge of nature that science actually seeks to discover were already complete. Thus, the only meaningful question to ask is how effective science is at discovering truths about the natural world *relative to some other method*. In such a case we could compare science to rival procedures such as common sense, superstition or old wives' tales and then set the evaluative bar at, say, our avoidance of sickness, injury and disease. Science would tell us, for example, that the white powder that we are considering to sweeten our tea with is actually salt, whereas our common sense understanding may interpret it to be sugar. The important point is that to make an argument in favour of science as the preferred method of discovery of truths about the world, we do not need it to tell us everything about that world in advance.

In the case of competition, to be sure, Hayek accepts that we are not asking how good it is as a method for uncovering facts that are assumed to be true of an invariant natural world. In contrast to the object of scientific enquiry, market competition is concerned with facts about the beliefs and knowledge of other people that are local and often transient and tacitly held. In contrast to science, then, where particular facts are sought in order to make true statements about the world, with competition we seek to discover facts about the state of the world, including people's wants and needs, as it is thought to be at a given time and place. This difference notwithstanding, at the level of the evaluation of scientific method and of competition as discovery procedures the problem is the same: if we could assume knowledge of all the facts of which competition actually makes use, we could then test its efficacy in objective terms. Now, this is precisely what economic theory's conception of 'perfect competition' is supposed to do by providing a yardstick with which we can measure the efficacy of markets. Where the yardstick is that of an 'equilibrium' state in which all the knowledge of local conditions has been communicated and resources have been allocated to their most productive use.[32]

However, as with scientific method, in reality we never do have this knowledge. For Hayek, therefore, the only sensible question to ask about the efficaciousness of markets is how good they are at communicating knowledge *relative to some other method* such as central planning.[33] What we can say here is that, given the Knowledge Problem, market competition is better than any known alternative because it makes better use of this knowledge.[34] Thus, he claims that

> it would be as easy to discredit the theory of scientific method by noting that it does not lead to verifiable predictions regarding what science will discover, as it has been to discredit the theory of the market by noting that it does not lead to predictions about particular outcomes of the market process.[35]

In both cases, however, to discredit the results of the processes they describe in this way would be nonsensical. Our criticisms of the market as not providing enough, or doing so chaotically, do not make much sense because they assume the achievement of an alternative scenario which is not possible. '[I]t is unfair to judge the performance of the market in a certain sense "from the top down"', Hayek writes, 'namely by comparing it with an ideal standard that we are unable to attain in any known way'.[36]

These insights have important implications for the argument we may make in favour of markets and their relationship to the neo-classical notion of perfect competition. 'The argument in favour of competition', Hayek writes in 'The Meaning of Competition', 'does not rest on the conditions that would exist if it were perfect'.[37] Indeed, the whole point of the market is that even in specific cases where, owing to the nature of the market in question, it could never reach a perfect competitive state of equilibrium, the important question is whether *any* alternative set of institutions could do this better. It is for this reason that Hayek considered the important political question to be not the extent to which actually existing markets match what could be achieved under conditions of perfect knowledge but, rather, to what extent different kinds of institutional arrangement respond to the Knowledge Problem.

Social Justice

Four criticisms of social justice

The idea that markets are all too often imperfect in the outcomes that they bring about is central not only to criticisms of views such as Hayek's but to arguments in favour of a more robust role for the state than we would consider Hayek to be in favour of. One important objection here is that institutions predicated on the enjoyment of individual liberty, particularly *economic* liberty, ignore the moral and political significance of poverty. Given diverse talents, it is inevitable that in a regime of individual economic freedom where equality is only accorded a formal status, there will be a sizeable number of people left behind in conditions of either relative or absolute poverty. The idea of poverty, the argument continues, is deeply troubling to most people and any society that allowed it to go unaddressed would be deeply unjust. The appropriate response to poverty and inequality, therefore, is not for the state to stand idly by but, rather, to guarantee positive welfare rights in addition to the formal rights associated with private property and free markets in the name of 'social justice'. Moreover, such a minimal role for the state is not something that Hayek can immediately dismiss because the state should take an active role in the securing of just economic outcomes without falling afoul of the problems that Hayek claims besets central planning. Social justice, then, falls on the acceptable side of the distinction between central planning and cultivation and is a nuanced response to the former's epistemological drawbacks to which thinkers such as Hayek should lend their support.

Disputes about social justice are at the centre of the distinction between 'classical' and 'egalitarian' varieties of liberalism in which epistemologically grounded theories such as Hayek's and, from a natural rights perspective, Nozick, are said to be at odds with those advanced by thinkers such as Rawls and Brian Barry who defend a direct economic role for the state.[38] Importantly, and despite the possibility that the pursuit of social justice is the kind of role for the state that Hayek should defend, his liberalism can be said to be 'classical' not only because of his positive epistemological defence of markets but also because of his critique of the idea of social justice itself. In *The Mirage of Social Justice* and other texts Hayek rejects social justice in two different ways by raising four objections to social justice centring first upon its meaninglessness and atavism as an *idea*, and second, upon its *practical* pursuit as unfeasible and incompatible with the liberal market order whose outcomes it seeks to correct.[39] To obtain a complete picture of his views on our proper stance towards the economy of a complex society we need now to look at this critique in detail.

The idea of social justice is meaningless

It is important to note at the outset that Hayek's claim about meaninglessness is not intended as a point about semantics but rather about the attribution or predication of justice – 'social,' or otherwise, to the catallactic outcomes of a free market economy because it falsely assumes that some identifiable agent deliberately brings them about.

He does concede 'that the manner in which the benefits and burdens are apportioned by the market mechanism would in many instances have to be regarded as very unjust *if* it were the result of a deliberate allocation to particular people'.[40] Hayek fully accepts that in a society in which shares were deliberately determined, it would follow that distribution ought to conform to a principle of justice such as equality, need or merit and that if we could deliberately coordinate the efforts of individuals to achieve a particular distribution then 'the question of how available means for the satisfaction of ends ought to be shared out becomes indeed a question of justice'.[41] In these cases, Hayek points out, 'a given set of means is allocated in accordance with a unitary plan among the competing ends according to their relative importance'.[42] Yet, as seen in his economic theory, the outcome of the catallactic process of the liberal market order cannot be deliberately brought about in this way. Unlike an organization, in the spontaneous order of the market '[t]here is no individual and no co-operating group of people against which the sufferer would have a just complaint'.[43]

To be sure, the problem Hayek highlights is not so much with the conception of social justice itself. It still *is* an appropriate conception insofar as the aggregate results of the actions of members of face-to-face communities or centrally planned economies are concerned. Nor is it that catallactic outcomes are not the products of intentional action. Such outcomes are overwhelmingly the results of intentional agency, but the important point is that the intentional agency in question is that of discrete individual agents acting at the disaggregated level under conditions of mutual ignorance and spatio-temporal distancing. Catallactic economic outcomes are indeed the direct results of intentional agency but are not the direct results of the intentional agency of a discrete *individual agent or group of them.* It is for this reason Hayek claims that rather than evaluate catallactic outcomes in terms of their social (in)justice, 'wholly different moral attitudes' are required towards the economic outcomes spontaneously yielded in the Great Society.[44] Therefore, for Hayek, justice

> clearly has no application to the manner in which the impersonal process of the market allocates command over goods and services to particular people: this can be neither just nor unjust, because the results are not intended nor foreseen, and depend on a multitude of circumstances not known in their totality to anybody.[45]

The idea of social justice is atavistic

Related to this critique about meaningfulness is Hayek's second claim that this idea of social justice is an atavistic throwback to a bygone age in which societies were sufficiently small for social interaction to be of a 'face-to-face' character. Precisely because in such societies it is possible to have direct knowledge of others' circumstances and of how one's actions impact upon them, justice claims *could* be meaningfully made about aggregate economic outcomes. This is possible because such societies have 'a unitary purpose, or a common hierarchy of ends, and a deliberate sharing of means according to a common view of individual merits'.[46] Because of this possibility in a face-to-face society we may meaningfully speak of the aggregate economic outcome being deliberately brought about and thus subject to the kind of ethical evaluations we ascribe to the behaviour of individuals themselves.

Matters are very different for Hayek when we predicate (in)justice of the aggregate outcome of a *catallactic* process. In this case we transpose the face-to-face conception of justice to the catallactic or extended order of the Great Society itself, as if there were a single agent or group who is able to self-consciously bring about the outcome in question. It is not surprising that we do this. 'As primitive thinking usually does when first noticing some regular process', Hayek writes,

> the results of the spontaneous ordering of the market were interpreted as if some thinking being deliberately directed them, or as if

the particular benefits or harm different persons derived from them were determined by deliberate acts of will, and could therefore be guided by moral rules as individual actions are.[47]

Thus, given the transposition of this intentionalist interpretation of complex social order and the idea of deliberate individual control it presupposes, it is only to be expected that there arises 'a demand that the members of society should organize themselves in a manner which makes it possible to assign particular shares of the product of society to the different individuals or groups' in conformity with principles that are morally attractive.[48] However, in a liberal market order this transposition is inappropriate because, as we saw with his first critique, there simply is no catallactic agent or group of agents who deliberately coordinate their efforts bring about the aggregate outcomes of the market.[49]

The pursuit of social justice is unfeasible

Despite these problems, Hayek acknowledges that the idea of social justice is nonetheless a very powerful one.[50] It is so powerful that we are motivated both as individuals and as political societies to pursue it. This notwithstanding, Hayek makes two related arguments in support of the claim that its pursuit, either by individuals or state agencies, can be neither successful nor yield a positive outcome. The individual pursuit of a socially just catallactic outcome is problematic for Hayek because, even if we assume a wholehearted altruism, as well as unanimity about which principle of social justice to adopt, the existence of the Knowledge Problem means that we would not know what to do in order to conform to it. There are no principles, he writes,

> by which the individual could so govern their conduct that in a Great Society the joint effect of their activities would be a distribution of benefits which could be described as materially just, or any other specific and intended allocation of advantages and disadvantages among particular people or groups.[51]

In contrast to a face-to-face community, in a complex society adherence to a principle of social justice would not tell us how to coordinate in order to achieve a socially just outcome. Moreover, the problem

Hayek identifies is compounded by the fact that each individual's standing in the catallactic order is not only determined by his own talents and abilities, as well as on occasion by exogenous events, but also by the multiplicity of decisions taken themselves under ever-changing circumstances by others, the vast majority of whom the individual is unaware of. Bringing about a socially just outcome is impossible, therefore, not only because in the complex and extended order of the Great Society knowledge of the results of agents' economic activities is never given, but also because that knowledge is constantly changing as a result of changes in objective circumstances and of previous decisions. Clearly even morally motivated agents are in no position to achieve social justice and that the individual economic agent 'cannot aim at just results if he does not know who will be affected'.[52]

The pursuit of social justice is incompatible with a liberal market economy

Given that in a complex society mutually ignorant individuals are in no position to bring about a socially just outcome, the alternative is for the state to do so. Yet, in Hayek's view the chances of this being a success are not particularly high. The reason for this relates to the discussion of the nature of the catallaxy and of the kinds of rules of just conduct which govern its operation. These rules are devoid of reference to particulars (including particular groups), and are universalizable prohibitions upon action rather than commands to undertake specific actions, thus they permit economic agents to decide for themselves what are, among a host of factors, the relevant moral criteria with respect to distribution. This end-state or *telos*-independent nature of the rules that govern the catallactic process, serves an important coordinative function in a world of dispersed, fleeting and tacit knowledge. By not being subject to specific commands but only to abstract, negative rules of just conduct, individuals enjoy personal sovereignty over economic decision-making and thus are not only able to exploit the knowledge they have of local circumstances but are also able to share that knowledge with largely unseen others through the price mechanism. In Hayek's system the question of which moral value or values should serve as the ultimate basis for economic distribution is not reflected by the rules of just conduct. Rather, these rules allow for the determination of questions of distributive fairness in a world of dispersed and tacit knowledge. For Hayek the question of appropriate moral values for distribution is a question that liberal institutions of state permit to be discovered rather than be politically second-guessed by the state itself.

By contrast, as an organization with a predetermined goal, if the state is to pursue social justice, content must be given as to what this amounts to so that roles and responsibilities may be arranged to achieve it. For Hayek, at the heart of any account of social justice is the idea that there is a single value – traditionally conceptualized in terms of desert, need, well-being or equality – by which the rules that govern economic intercourse are justified and operate. But, crucially, for Hayek this brings a host of difficulties because it is not possible to formulate an enforceable rule of just individual conduct that satisfied both social justice and the demand that it allow for the emergence of prices to act as signals that tell us what needs to be done with resources.[53] Hayek is sure to point out, however, that this does not mean that values are irrelevant to the determination of catallactic shares. Rather,

> [t]he prices which must be paid in a market economy for different kinds of labour and other factors of production if individual efforts are to match, although they will be affected by effort, diligence, skill, need, etc., cannot conform to any *one* of these magnitudes; and considerations of justice just do not make sense with respect to the determination of a magnitude which does not depend on anyone's skill or desire, but on circumstances which nobody knows in their totality.[54]

Thus, just as the pursuit of social justice in a catallaxy is unfeasible at the individual level because nobody would have the complete knowledge required to direct resources to their socially just use, Hayek claims that at the level of the state it would unavoidably impede the functioning of the very mechanism needed for us to have *any* idea about what to do with resources, even if there were political consensus about the just purpose for which we wish to employ them.

In any case, the devolution of the pursuit of social justice to the state does not free it from the necessities that Hayek claims constrain the actions of individual market participants. This is significant, for it is where the connection between the absence of a price mechanism, compulsion and the incompatibility of social justice with a market economy becomes clear. Given that, in a world of limited resources the inescapable need to make *some* kind of decision about resource alloca-tion so as to achieve a socially just outcome and given that in a world marked by spatio-temporal distancing, individuals would not know all that they would need to know to achieve it, Hayek claims that the state would have no choice but to tell them.[55] In an important respect, then, there is a fundamental equivalence between the two processes. On the one hand in the market decisions about what needs to be done are in large part 'taken' by the price mechanism under a regime where people enjoy freedom of contract but where, due to what Hayek calls the 'impersonal compulsion' of the market process, they have an infin-itesimally small degree of personal control over the economic context in which they must act.[56] By contrast, in the case of the state individu-als are freed from the impositions of the price mechanism but only at the cost of their being directly told what to do so that a socially just outcome may be achieved.[57] For Hayek, the choice between the mar-ket and the socially just state becomes not one between freedom and tyranny but between impersonal and personal compulsion.

Equally significant is the fact that in their pursuit of social justice state actors would nonetheless have to make decisions under the con-ditions identified by the Knowledge Problem, and that they would be driven in no small measure by values of expediency and efficiency rather than social justice itself. Thus, not only would state agents have to issue commands to individuals, but do so on an *ad hoc* basis as changes in circumstances dictated. Again, the choice between the market order and state pursuit of social justice is not a choice between inequality and equality but, rather between two kinds of inequality. 'No less than in the market order', Hayek writes, 'would the individu-als in the common interest have to submit to great inequality – only these inequalities would be determined not by the interaction of individual skills in an impersonal process, but by the uncontradict-able decision of authority'.[58] For Hayek the choice is simple in both cases. Being commanded what to do is indeed worse than having the economic nexus at large act as the constraining context upon one's decisions, not least because it stifles rather than allows for the co-ordination of the social knowledge that is an inescapable prereq-uisite for rational economic decision-making of any kind in a com-plex society.

It is here that Hayek's unfeasibility and incompatibility arguments are connected. Precisely because of the Knowledge Problem of the 'necessary and irremediable ignorance on everyone's part of most of the particular facts which determine the actions of all the several members of human society' the state would inevitably find itself forced to adopt an ever more interventionist stance to make up for its failure to achieve the distributive outcome it desired.[59] Doing so, however, would ultimately transform the catallaxy, if not into a Soviet-style command economy, then into an *economy of commands* where the pursuit of social justice 'must progressively approach nearer and nearer to a totalitarian system'.[60]

Hayek's minimal safety net concession

Space does not permit study of the cogency of Hayek's criticisms in any depth, although there is a significant literature on this.[61] It is significant, nevertheless, that despite them, Hayek ultimately defends a direct role for the state in the provision of an economic minimum. In 'The Principles of a Liberal Social Order' he claims that '[t]here is of course no reason why a society which, thanks to the market, is as rich as modern society should not provide *outside the market* a minimum security for all who in the market fall below a certain standard'.[62] Given that Hayek also rejects the 'government doing what is required in order to place the different citizens in equal (or less unequal) material positions', it is difficult for him to sustain the minimum safety net concession for at least two reasons.[63] Firstly, assuring a minimum income for those who are unable to earn an adequate one in the market is, whilst perhaps laudable, to ensure that citizens are placed in a less unequal position than they would otherwise find themselves in. Secondly, and perhaps most importantly, diverting resources in this way would conflict deeply with Hayek's epistemological claim about the coordinative function of markets. Diverting resources to places other than those where they would have ended up in a catallactic process is to just hinder individuals from exploiting their own and others' knowledge and, with it, the process by which knowledge is utilized by society at large so that resources end up going to where they will be used most effectively.

There is, furthermore, an epistemological problem with Hayek's concession that places it sharply at odds with the epistemological underpinnings of the feasibility and compatibility arguments. Even if ethical unanimity with respect to direct state provision of a minimum is conceded for the sake of argument, without institutions which allow it to be discovered, there will be no mechanism for knowing whether any centralized political determination of the relevant minimum is the appropriate one, even if there is agreement about it. Indeed, it is quite possible that such a determination may actually *under*determine the minimum as it would be incapable of taking into consideration all the relevant factors that would need to be known to ensure that it is adequate, including not only levels of poverty, but also of the sources and social processes that lead to poverty. Even more problematically and given that the determination process would be subject to the monopoly power of the state in this way, there would be no means of verifying that such an underdetermination had taken place nor, even if this were not an issue, of changing the minimum in a timely manner, once negative feedback started to come through in the form of increased or stubbornly persistent rates of poverty. Thus, in defending the centralized political determination and delivery of an economic minimum, Hayek appears to be falling victim to the very epistemological problems he identifies with the determination of any economic question of value outside of the market. The whole point of the market process is precisely to determine just these kinds of question in a manner that is responsive to the fact of dispersed and tacit knowledge of localized differences and of mutual ignorance and spatio-temporal distancing between economic agents. Given that these are universal features of the epistemological problem that he identifies, the onus is surely on Hayek here to demonstrate why they would not present insurmountable problems for the centralized determination and implementation of a statutory economic minimum.

Finally, Hayek claims that not only is the direct state provision of a minimum prudential, it 'may be felt to be *a clear moral duty of all* to assist, within the organized community, those who cannot help themselves'.[64] As laudable as such a duty may be, it nevertheless reveals on Hayek's part not only an inconsistency with his epistemological critiques of the centralized pursuit of social justice, but also with his spontaneous order-based meaninglessness and atavism critiques. As Steven Lukes points out, according to Hayek's own arguments

[o]ne's inability to earn an adequate income is surely either one's own doing or the 'fault' of the market order in which one finds oneself, not the doing of those Hayek would force to remedy the situation. It appears, therefore, that Hayek concedes that people may have obligations to help each other even when those so obliged did not cause the distress to be alleviated – indeed, when this distress is the result of an impersonal, spontaneous order.[65]

This admission of an obligation on the part of the state to aid the least well-off, despite their situation *not* being the result of the deliberate, coordinated action of others, creates a very deep problem for Hayek's position. If social justice claims about the overall results of the catallactic process are atavistic and meaningless, why, if not as a matter of justice, does Hayek think it necessary to compel all members of society to help the less well-off when according to the spontaneous order-based theory of the catallaxy they have no direct culpability in their situation? The onus is surely on Hayek to show how this obligation of justice is not sourced in the same meaningless and atavistic sentiment he claims plagues the description of catallactic outcomes as unjust. Given these difficulties and the deeper trouble Hayek would find himself in if he were to adopt a natural rights-based approach such as Nozick's, his only options are to withdraw the concession and extend his critique, as has been claimed, 'even to the provision of a minimal safety net,' and/or theorize a role for the state in the reduction of economic inequality that is more consistent with his epistemological liberal premises.[66] Neither of these options, however, were taken up by him.

Notes

[1] Hayek, F. A., 'The Use of Knowledge in Society', in Hayek, F. A. (ed.), *Individualism and Economic Order*, Chicago, IL, University of Chicago Press, (1945) 1948, p. 77. See also Hayek, *The Counter-Revolution of Science: Studies in the Abuse of Reason*, Indianapolis, IN, Liberty Fund, 1952b, pp. 91–92, 165–182; 'The Facts of the Social Sciences', in Hayek, F.A. (ed.), *Individualism and Economic Order*, Chicago, IL, University of Chicago Press, (1942) 1948, pp. 69–72.

[2] Walras, L., *Elements of Pure Economics*, London, Routledge, (1874) 2003.

[3] Hayek, F. A., 'The Meaning of Competition', in Hayek, *Individualism and Economic Order*, Chicago, IL, University of Chicago Press, (1946b) 1948, pp. 92–106.

[4] Hayek, F. A., 'Economics and Knowledge', in Hayek, F. A., *Individualism and Economic Order*, Chicago, IL, University of Chicago Press, (1936) 1948, p. 35.

[5] ibid., p. 46.

[6] Hayek, 'Use of Knowledge in Society', p. 91.

[7] Hayek, 'The Meaning of Competition', p. 94.

[8] Hayek, 'Use of Knowledge in Society', pp. 90–91.

[9] Mises, L., *Human Action*, Yale, CT, Yale University Press, 1949, chapter 14, §5.

10 Hayek, 'The Meaning of Competition', p. 101.

11 Mises, L., *Socialism*, Indianapolis, IN, Liberty Fund, (1922) 1981. p. 105; Zamyatin, Y., *We*, New York, NY, EOS Publishing, (1921) 1999, p. 24.

12 Hayek, 'Economics and Knowledge', p. 54.

13 Hayek, 'The Meaning of Competition', p. 93.

14 See Hayek, 'Economics and Knowledge', p. 35; 'The Meaning of Competition', p. 93.

15 Hayek, F. A., 'Socialist Calculation III: *The Competitive "Solution"*', in Hayek, F. A. (ed.), *Individualism and Economic Order*, Chicago, IL, University of Chicago Press, (1940) 1948, pp. 181–182; *The Counter Revolution of Science*, p. 75; 'Use of Knowledge in Society' p. 90; Hayek, F. A., 'The Economy, Science and Politics', in Hayek, F. A. (ed.), *Studies in Philosophy, Politics and Economics*, London, Routledge and Kegan Paul, (1963) 1967, pp. 261; 'The Theory of Complex Phenomena', p. 35.

16 Hayek, 'Economics and Knowledge', p. 33.

17 Hayek, *The Road to Serfdom*, Chicago, IL, University of Chicago Press, (1944) 1976, p. 20; *The Counter-Revolution of Science*, pp. 141–182, esp. pp. 141, 148, 161–162; 'Individualism: True and False', in Hayek, F. A. (ed.), *Individualism and Economic Order*, Chicago, IL, University of Chicago Press, (1946a) 1948,§§5–11; 'Freedom and the Economic System', in Caldwell, B. (ed.) *Socialism and War: Essays, Documents, Reviews*, in *The Collected Works of F. A. Hayek*, vol. 10, Chicago, IL, University of Chicago Press, (1939) 1997, pp. 189–211.

18 Caldwell, *Hayek's Challenge*, pp. 241. See also *The Counter-Revolution of Science*, p. 162, n. 10.

19 This article was originally published in german and appeared in translation in Hayek, *Collectivist Economic Planning: Critical Studies on The Possibilities Of Socialism*, pp. 87–130; See also Mises, *Socialism*. Conclusions very similar to Mises' were also reached independently by Max Weber and the Russian economist Boris Brutzkus. On this see Hayek 'The Nature and History of the Problem', pp. 32–35. For a review of Mises' contribution see Steele, D. R. *From Marx to Mises: Post-Capitalist Society and the Challenge of Economic Calculation*, La Salle, Open Court, 1992.

20 Mises, 'Economic Calculation in the Socialist Commonwealth', in Hayek, F.A. (ed.), *Collectivist Economic Planning: Critical Studies on The Possibilities Of Socialism*, Auburn, AL, The Ludwig von Mises Institute, (1920) 2009, p. 110.

21 Hayek, *Rules and Order*, London, Routledge, 1973, p.12, emphasis added.

22 Hayek, 'The Economy, Science and Politics', p. 263.

23 Hayek, 'Use of Knowledge in Society', p. 77.

24 Hayek, F. A., 'The Nature and History of the Problem', in Hayek, F. A. (ed.), *Collectivist Economic Planning: Critical Studies on The Possibilities Of Socialism*, Auburn, Ludwig von Mises Institute, (1935) 2009, pp. 4–6.

25 Hayek, 'Use of Knowledge in Society', p.77.

26 Ibid., p. 77.

27 Kukathas, *Hayek and Modern Liberalism*, Oxford, Clarendon Press, 1989, p. 57. See also Lavoie, D., *Rivalry and Central Planning*, Cambridge, Cambridge University Press, 1985. Boettke, P. J.,'Hayek and Market Socialism', in Feser, E. (ed.), *The Cambridge Companion to Hayek*, Cambridge, Cambridge University Press, 2006, pp. 60–61. John O' Neill makes a similar survey of

the early part of the Socialist calculation debate between Neurath and Mises in O'Neill, J., 'Who won the Socialist Calculation Debate?', *History of Political Thought*, vol. XVII, no. 3, Autumn 1996, p. 442.

[28] Hayek, 'The Confusion of Language in Political Thought', pp. 90–91; *The Mirage of Social Justice*, pp. 107–132; *The Political Order of a Free People*, London, Routledge, 1979, pp. 65–77.

[29] Hayek, 'Competition as a Discovery Procedure', *The Quarterly Journal of Austrian Economics*, vol. 5, no. 3, (1968b) 2002, p. 9. See also Hayek, *The Political Order of a Free People*, pp. 67–68.

[30] Locke, J., *Two Treatises of Government*, Cambridge, Cambridge University Press, (1690) 2005, chapter 5.

[31] Hayek, 'Competition as a Discovery Procedure', p. 10; *The Political Order of a Free People*, p. 68.

[32] Hayek, 'The Meaning of Competition', p. 94.

[33] Hayek, 'Competition as a Discovery Procedure', p. 10; *The Political Order of a Free People*, p. 68.

[34] Hayek, 'The Economy, Science, and Politics', p. 262; *The Political Order of a Free People*, p. 68.

[35] Hayek, 'Competition as a Discovery Procedure', p. 11. See also Hayek, 'The Meaning of Competition', p. 105.

[36] Ibid., p. 16; *The Political Order of a Free People*, p. 68. See also Hayek, 'The Meaning of Competition', p. 100.

[37] Hayek, 'The Meaning of Competition', p. 104; *The Political Order of a Free People*, pp. 65–67.

[38] See Nozick, *Anarchy, State and Utopia* New York, Basic Books, 1974; Rawls, *A Theory of Justice*, Oxford, Oxford University Press, 1971; Barry, B., *Why Social Justice Matters*, Cambridge , Polity Press, 2005.

[39] Hayek, *The Political Ideal of the Rule of Law*, Cairo, National Bank of Egypt, 1955a, pp. 47–49; Hayek, F. A., 'What is "Social"? – What Does it Mean?', in Hayek, F. A. (ed.), *Studies in Philosophy, Politics and Economics*, London, Routledge and Kegan Paul, (1957/1961) 1967, pp. 237–247; *The Mirage of Social Justice*, pp. 62–132; Hayek, F. A., 'The Atavism of Social Justice', in Hayek, F. A. (ed.), *New Studies in Philosophy, Politics, Economic and the History of Ideas*, London, Routledge and Kegan Paul, (1976c) 1978, pp. 57–68.

[40] Hayek, *The Mirage of Social Justice*, p. 64.

[41] Ibid., pp. 64, 81.

[42] Ibid., p. 107.

[43] Ibid., pp. 69, 108.

[44] Hayek, 'The Atavism of Social Justice', p. 61.

[45] Hayek, *The Mirage of Social Justice*, p. 70. See also Hayek, 'Economic Freedom and Representative Government', in Hayek, F.A. (ed.), *New Studies in Philosophy, Politics, Economics and the History of Ideas*, London, Routledge and Kegan Paul, (1973b) 1978, p. 110.

[46] Hayek, 'The Atavism of Social Justice', p. 59. See also Hayek, *The Mirage of Social Justice*, pp. 88–91, chapter 10.

[47] Hayek, *The Mirage of Social Justice*, p. 62. See also Hayek, *The Political Ideal of the Rule of Law*, p. 30.

[48] Ibid., p. 64.

[49] Ibid., pp. 42, 62.
[50] Ibid., pp. 65–67.
[51] Ibid., p. 85. See also Ibid. pp. 78, 83–84.
[52] Ibid., p. 90.
[53] Ibid., p. 120, see also Ibid., p. 80.
[54] Ibid., p. 80, emphasis added.
[55] Ibid., pp. 82–83.
[56] Hayek, 'Competition as a Discovery Procedure', p. 189.
[57] Hayek, *The Road to Serfdom*, p. 92.
[58] Hayek, *The Mirage of Social Justice*, p. 83. See also Hayek, *The Political Ideal of the Rule of Law*, pp. 47–49.
[59] Hayek, *Rules and Order*, p. 12.
[60] Hayek, *The Mirage of Social Justice*, p. 68. See also Hayek, *The Road to Serfdom; The Constitution of Liberty*, pp. 231–232.
[61] Feser, E., 'Hayek on Social Justice: Reply to Lukes and Johnston', *Critical Review*, vol. 11, no. 4 (Fall 1997), pp. 581–606; Lukes, S., *Liberals and Cannibals*, London, Verso Press, 2003, pp. 117–131; Plant, R., 'Hayek on Social Justice: A Critique', in J. Birner and R. van Zijp (eds), *Hayek, Co-ordination and Evolution*, London, Routledge, 1994, pp. 175–176; Tebble, A. J., 'Hayek and Social Justice: A Critique', *Critical Review of International Social and Political Philosophy*, vol. 13, no. 4, 2009, pp. 581–604. See also Burczak, T., *Socialism after Hayek*, Ann Arbor, University of Michigan Press, 2006.
[62] Hayek, 'The Principles of a Liberal Social order', in Hayek, F.A. (ed.), *Studies in Philosophy, Politics and Economics*, London, Routledge and Kegan Paul, (1966) 1967, p. 175; See also Hayek, *The Road to Serfdom*, pp. 120, 132; *The Constitution of Liberty*, pp. 257, 285–286; 'Liberalism', p. 145; The *Mirage of Social Justice*, pp. 87, 139, 1978; 'Economic Freedom and Representative Government', p. 114; Hayek, F. A., '"Free" Enterprise and Competitive Order', in Hayek, F. A. (ed.), *Individualism and Economic Order*, Chicago, IL, University of Chicago Press, (1947) 1948, p. 112; *Hayek on Hayek*, pp. 148–149.
[63] Hayek, *The Mirage of Social Justice*, p. 82.
[64] Ibid., p. 87, emphasis added.
[65] Lukes, S., *Liberals and Cannibals*, London, Verso Press, 2003, p. 124.
[66] Feser, 'Hayek on Social Justice: Reply to Lukes and Johnston', p. 597.

4

Political and Legal Theory

Hayek's Liberalism

Epistemology and the circumstances of justice

We have seen that Hayek rejects centralized economic planning and social justice and defends instead an account of the catallactic, or market, order and of the idea of the state as the cultivator, but not director, of the environment in which the specific outcomes of that order emerge. Despite this, his project remains incomplete in at least two respects. Firstly, in the texts we have examined thus far, he not only wishes to describe but actually to *recommend* certain kinds of institutions over others. Hayek needs to offer an argument as to why the classical liberal account of political association he so clearly favours should be preferred to others. Secondly, up until this point he has been overwhelmingly concerned with issues of *economic* coordination and of the distribution and allocation of resources. Economics, however, does not exhaust the domain of political theory, even if it may be of vital importance, because, as we saw towards the end of Chapter 2, he only sketches in the briefest of forms, in texts such as *The Road to Serfdom* and 'Individualism: True and False', the contours of this economic liberalism. In order to complete his political project and give specific substance and content to his idea of the cultivating role of the State, therefore, Hayek needs an account of *justice* that takes him beyond merely economic considerations.

Key texts in this regard are *The Constitution of Liberty* and the three volumes that constitute *Law, Legislation and Liberty: Rules and Order, The Mirage of Social Justice* and *The Political Order of a Free People*. Out of these works, and of individual papers that deal with similar themes, arise three important concerns with which Hayek would be preoccupied in his political theory subsequent to the publication of *The Road to*

Serfdom. Firstly, from his epistemological argument about the nature of social knowledge in complex societies and of the faculty of reason of those who are members of them, Hayek recasts the fundamental task of and rationale for justice in epistemological, rather than moral, terms, just as he had done earlier with regard to economic theory and practice. This reformulation, of course, is crucial to his now political purposes because it serves as the basis upon which he grounds his liberal commitment to individual freedom. Secondly, and related to this, he defends the idea of the protected individual domain and its economic corollary of private property rights. Thirdly, and to provide more substantive content to the idea of the protected individual domain, Hayek defends a theory of law and, more specifically, a theory of the *rule of law* as central to his liberal project.

It should be no surprise that, owing to the internal nature of the relationship he takes to exist between a complex society and the Knowledge Problem, this problem is also the focal point of Hayek's political project. Thus, at the centre of his thinking about justice, as in his social and economic theory, is what Hayek takes to be the epistemological foundation of justice itself. Looking back at his work of the preceding decades in the paper 'Kinds of Rationalism', Hayek explains that in 'Economics and Knowledge' he had examined 'the central difficulties of pure economic theory' and concluded that its main task was to explain how knowledge was acquired and communicated without ever being concentrated in a single mind.[1] Yet, he also conceded that it was still a great distance from this explanation

> to an adequate insight into the relations between the abstract rules which the individual follows in his actions, and the abstract overall order which is formed as a result of his responding, within the limits imposed upon him by those abstract rules, to the concrete particular circumstances which he encounters.[2]

Indeed, Hayek goes on to say that it is only at this point that he has reached what seems to be 'a tolerably clear picture of the nature of the spontaneous order of which liberal economists have so long been talking'.[3] This, of course, was a preoccupation that went right back to the earlier part of his career as an economist where he claims that '[t]he problem which we meet here is by no means peculiar to economics and arises in connection with nearly all truly social phenomena, with language and with most of our cultural inheritance, and

constitutes the central problem of all social science'.[4] Thus, we are
told that 'Economics and Knowledge' was 'the starting point' and the
reason 'why though at one time a very pure and narrow economic
theorist, [he] was led from technical economics into all kinds of questions usually regarded as philosophical'.[5] Similarly, and again referring
to 'Economics and Knowledge' as well as to 'The Use of Knowledge in
Society', Hayek comments in *Rules and Order*, that '[t]he insight into
the significance of our institutional ignorance in the economic sphere,
and into the methods by which we have learned to overcome this obstacle, was in fact the starting point for...ideas...systematically applied
to a much wider field'.[6] Just as he identified the principal problematic
of social theory to be to account for the existence of complex social
order in the light of the Knowledge Problem, Hayek would later claim
that the subjectively given nature of social knowledge 'is the source of
the central problem of all social order' and 'the reason why most social
institutions have taken the form they actually have'.[7]

What does Hayek's Knowledge Problem imply for his political rather
than economic theory? Importantly, he claims that similar to his discussion of the economic problem, '[a]ny examination of the moral
or legal order which leaves this fact out of account misses the central
problem'.[8] Indeed, the very possibility of justice 'rests on this necessary limitation of our factual knowledge, and that insight into the
nature of justice is therefore denied to all those constructivists who
habitually agree on the assumption of omniscience'.[9] '[I]n a society
of omniscient persons,' he continues, 'there would be no room for a
conception of justice: every action would have to be judged as a means
of bringing about known effects, and omniscience would presumably
include knowledge of the relative importance of the different effects'.[10]
Of course, it is precisely because we do *not* have this knowledge that we
need rules of justice to solve these problems. Thus, Hayek is moved to
claim that, rather than defend a substantive or end-state account of justice of 'known effects', political theory must be concerned with offering an account of how we discover which outcomes are optimal, given
our mutual ignorance and thoroughly social natures. More specifically, just because for epistemological reasons no individual is ever in a
position authoritatively to claim what an optimal specific economic or
social outcome for society as a whole would be, nor, even if this were
known, what specific decisions the achievement of such an outcome
would practically require, we must view justice as an answer to the
Knowledge Problem rather than as a question. That is, for Hayek the

task of justice is to secure the conditions for the discovery rather than imposition of social and economic *optima*.

This conception points us to the uniqueness of Hayek's position with regard to the fundamental rationale of justice. It is, indeed, a position which places him squarely outside of the mainstream of political theory. To get an idea of just how unique Hayek's conception of justice is, it will be useful to contrast it with the mainstream view of what are called the circumstances of justice. The circumstances of justice are typically described as those fundamental facts about us and about the world which explain our need for justice. According to the mainstream view as represented by thinkers such as David Hume and, in our own time, John Rawls, the circumstances of justice are comprised of two basic elements. The first circumstance is said to be objective in that it refers to a fact about the world that is independent of what we think or desire, whilst the second, subjective, circumstance refers to a truth about our collective moral life. For Hume, the objective circumstance of justice is that of the moderate scarcity of resources and the subjective circumstance is that of our limited beneficence.[11] The fact of moderate resource scarcity refers to the idea that resources are neither so abundant as to make the conflicts that give rise to the need for just decisions about how they should be allocated non-existent, nor so scarce that cooperative arrangements in virtue of which these disputes are settled are impossible to make. Similarly, with respect to limited beneficence, if we were wholly altruistic there would be no need for justice as we would only have the interests and needs of our fellows rather than ourselves in mind. At the other extreme, if we were only ever rapaciously self-interested, the very idea of justice would be nonsensical, premised as it is on our acceptance of adjudications of disputes emerging from our differing interests and conceptions of right and wrong, rather than on perpetual and irresolvable conflict.

Following Hume, Rawls also describes two circumstances of justice. The objective circumstance that makes justice both necessary and possible is the moderate scarcity of resources. In contrast to Hume, however, Rawls describes the subjective circumstance as that of disagreement about ends.[12] Thus, for Rawls it is not that we are partial and relatively less interested in the fortunes of those beyond our immediate circle but, rather, that we *disagree* about the ends of life that we should pursue. This means that we find it hard to agree on a set of rules which arbitrate our social intercourse, including intercourse about resource use. Conversely, then, we may assume that there would be no need for justice if circumstances were different and that there was unanimity about ends. Taken together these circumstances make justice both possible and desirable. Justice, that is, responds to the problem of limited resources amongst people who are partial or who disagree.

With respect to the objective circumstance of justice, Hayek follows Hume and Rawls. Were it not for moderate resource scarcity there would be no need for justice because everybody would have more than enough of what they needed and, as such, would not be in resource conflict with one another. Yet, importantly, Hayek differs from the mainstream of political philosophy with regard to the subjective circumstance of justice. Importantly, however, it is not that Hayek takes issue with the *content* of these subjective circumstances. Whether we are limited in our beneficence or disagree about the ends of life is largely irrelevant to his political concern. For Hayek, neither the Humean nor Rawlsian subjective circumstance of justice fully explains the rationale for justice. To be sure, this is not because they possibly mischaracterize the truth about our moral existence but, rather, precisely because the circumstances they point to are subjective and ethical in nature. Put another way, for Hayek the two circumstances that explain the rationale for justice are *both* objective in nature and facts about our ethical circumstances do not explain the need for justice.

With respect to Hume it is for Hayek, the epistemological fact of our permanently limited *knowledge* – whereby each and every one of us is only ever possessed of a portion of all the knowledge necessary for society to make rational economic decisions – rather than the truncated nature of our affections, that along with moderate resource scarcity, explains our need for justice. '[T]he possibility of justice', he writes, 'rests on [the] necessary *limitation* of our factual knowledge, and that insight into the nature of justice is therefore denied to all those constructivists who habitually argue on the assumption of omniscience'.[13] We can see how this is so by strengthening the Humean claim about limited beneficence to one about complete altruism where we are only ever concerned with the needs of others. Even here, Hayek points out, we would still not be in a position to satisfy needs because the knowledge of them and of the resource availabilities and productive possibilities relevant to their satisfaction is never given to a single mind. Thus, even in a far more benevolent world than the one Hume actually describes, we would still need some kind of just decision-making mechanism to decide which limited resources should go to whom, how they should be allocated and in what quantity. As Hayek claimed in *The Mirage of Social Justice* there is 'no possibility for the individual to know what he would have to do to secure a just remuneration of his fellows'.[14]

Similarly, with respect to Rawls and disagreement, even if there were unanimity with respect to ends of life, the fact of our irremediable ignorance would still mean that we needed justice to coordinate the knowledge relevant to their achievement. That is, even if we assumed unanimity about ends, we would still in any case be faced with the question of knowing what it is that we – as both individuals and as a society – ought to do in order to satisfy the demands pursuit of those ends placed upon us. Thus, regardless of whether we imagine ourselves to be only partially or wholly beneficent, or only ever in disagreement or complete agreement about the ends of life, the fact of the Knowledge Problem means that, in either case, we are never in a position to know all that we would need to know in order to attend to the needs of our overwhelmingly unseen fellows in complex or, as Hume put it, 'large' societies.[15] Thus, it is not so much the subjective circumstance of limited beneficence and disagreement about ends coupled with the objective circumstances of moderate resource scarcity that is important. Rather it is the objective circumstances of moderate resource scarcity and the Knowledge Problem that explains our need for justice. The fundamental question that Hayek's perspective orients us towards is not: *how should benefits and burdens be arranged in a world of limited resources,* and of *limited beneficence or endemic disagreement?* Rather, it is *which institutions of justice allow for the discovery of how benefits and burdens ought to be distributed under conditions of limited resources and knowledge?*

The knowledge problem and liberal individualism

Given that for Hayek justice is a procedure for the discovery of answers to economic and social questions rather than an institutional instantiation of any particular substantive answer itself, it becomes necessary to ascertain just *who* is to do the discovering and on what basis. As we saw in Chapter 2, Hayek claims that individualism is primarily a social theory and 'only in the second instance a set of political maxims derived from this view of society'.[16] This notwithstanding, it is clear that, upon the basis of the Knowledge Problem, Hayek derives the maxim that constitutes at the most basic level his normative political theory: that individuals enjoy a clearly delimited and inviolable sphere of *freedom* in which they may act upon their particular knowledges.[17] Moreover, in the economic sphere, for Hayek they are able to do so only if there is established certain general commitments to the institution of private property and to the idea of consent with respect to property's acquisition and transfer. In other words, individuals in the complex order should have 'a known sphere of things which we can control and which we call his property, and that these things can be transferred from the sphere of one to that of another only by mutual consent'.[18] This, of course, is Hayek's argument for private property rights whose rationale is that they 'tell each what he can count upon, what material objects or services he can use for his purposes, and what is the range of actions open to him'.[19]

Hayek offers three arguments for his liberal individualism. The first takes the consequences of the Knowledge Problem for the individual as primary, another focuses on the epistemological consequences for society of the enjoyment of individual liberty and a third is based upon the relationship between the ends of life that we pursue and the means at our disposal for doing so. The first, individualist, argument arises from the universal nature of the Knowledge Problem that lies at the heart of what we have characterized as the Hayekian circumstances of justice. Because we are only ever acquainted with different parts of society's stock of knowledge, the only way in which that knowledge can be made use of adequately is if we all enjoy the liberty to decide what to do for ourselves. 'We want the individual to have liberty', Hayek writes, 'because only if he can decide what to do can he also use all his unique combination of information, skills and capacities which nobody else can fully appreciate'.[20] The second argument is that individual liberty thus constituted enables *society* as a whole to achieve more than would otherwise be the case. More specifically, the conferral of individual liberty enables us to make greater use of otherwise socially unavailable dispersed, fleeting and tacit knowledge in comparison to regimes that do not privilege individual decision-making to as great an extent. As he says in *The Constitution of Liberty* when discussing the process by which society exploits its stock of knowledge,

> [w]hat is essential to the functioning of the process is that each individual be able to act on his particular knowledge, always unique, at

least so far as it refers to some particular circumstances, and that he be able to use his individual skills and opportunities within the limits known to him and for his own individual purpose.[21]

Thus, given that the knowledge necessary to affect social coordination is scattered among individuals the only way in which it may be utilized is via allowing individual freedom. The extent to which public institutions do this is the extent to which society will be adept at exploiting its stock of individually held but socially constituted knowledge.

Freedom of action as freedom of conscience

An important question at this juncture concerns the kinds of activity the individual freedom that Hayek defends is supposed to protect. In line with standard accounts such as that of J. S. Mill, it protects in the first instance freedom of thought, expression and conscience.[22] Indeed, given Hayek's epistemological perspective, it would be reasonable to conclude that these most thoroughly 'epistemological' freedoms, concerned as they are with expressing and sharing what we know and what we believe about the world would be the most important freedoms of all. Yet, Hayek contends that in an important sense freedom of thought and liberty of conscience and expression alone are but empty and formal, if not impotent, freedoms unless accompanied by individual freedom of *action*. Indeed, given the centrality that we saw in the previous chapter he attaches to the exploitation of dispersed, transient and tacit knowledge in the economic discovery process, individual freedom of action is in a significant sense *prior to* freedom of thought and liberty of conscience and expression in Hayek's political theory.

Thus, whilst being of central importance, the exercise of liberty of conscience and freedom of expression are for Hayek 'only the *last* stage of the process in which new truths are discovered' and out of which arises the explicit, propositional knowledge that we are able to discuss.[23] Indeed, he continues, it is from the utilization of tacit knowledge via action that the economic discovery process gains its creative potential: 'the flow of new ideas', he writes, 'springs from the sphere in which *action*, often *non-rational* action, and material events impinge upon one another' and which, 'would dry up if freedom were confined to the intellectual sphere'.[24] It is for this reason that

Hayek claims in *The Constitution of Liberty* that '[t]o extol the value of intellectual liberty at the expense of the value of liberty of doing things would be like treating the crowning part of an edifice as the whole'.[25] To only confer intellectual liberty rather than, we may say, freedom of action, concerning distribution would be to thoroughly impoverish the epistemological basis upon which social decisions concerning distribution would be arrived at. Furthermore, his reasoning relates in an important way to his commitment to private property. For Hayek, the freedom to dispose of and actively choose amongst economic means is how economic coordination in a complex society is actually achieved in a rational way.[26] The absence of individual economic freedom, then, is *au fond* the marker of irrational economic decision-making.

Whilst accepting that it may be through the institution of the liberal market economy that we make use of dispersed, fleeting and tacit social knowledge in a complex society, one could nevertheless object that Hayek's is ultimately a severely limited conception of justice that omits important, non-economic, considerations. This, of course, is something of which Hayek is aware when, in *The Constitution of Liberty*, he claims that 'freedom of action is wider than the concept of "economic liberty"'. Indeed, he questions whether restrictions upon liberty can be confined to the economic sphere at all because '[e]conomic considerations are merely those by which we *reconcile* and *adjust* our different purposes, none of which, in the last resort, are economic'.[27] This relates directly to a third argument that Hayek offers in favour of individual economic liberty. Given that it is our reason that chooses the ends that we seek to pursue, the realization of those ends, he writes, 'depends on the availability of the required means'.[28] Because of this relationship of dependency of the realization of ends upon our means to realize them, control of the means to our ends ultimately entails control over the ends that one may choose. Without the freedom to dispose of the economic means as we see fit in the pursuit of our ends – that is, without private property – the freedom to pursue ends is emptied of any significance and becomes a merely formal freedom. As he argues in 'Liberalism', '[t]here can be no freedom of press if the instruments of printing are under government control, no freedom of assembly if the needed rooms are so controlled, no freedom of movement if the means of transport are a government monopoly'.[29] This problem is made more interesting precisely because the charge of the classical liberal regime protecting merely formal, and quite possibly worthless, rights and liberties is often raised against it by those who seek to defend a more expansive role for the state.[30]

Another important objection to Hayek's liberal conception is that it ignores the potential for private companies to exert similar powers of control over individuals via ownership of the means of production. Hayek is right, then, that there can be no freedom of assembly if all the meeting rooms are publicly owned, but that would also be true if they were owned by the same company. He therefore needs to provide an explanation for his specific focus upon the potential dangers to individual liberty of state ownership. The explanation for this takes us back to his arguments about the appropriate bases of evaluation of differing political and economic systems that we examined in the previous chapter. Whilst not denying that the existence of private monopoly presents problems which need to be addressed, Hayek claims that it makes little sense to object to it on the basis that it would not do away with all the power relationships that come with the possibility of monopoly control. As with his discussion of catallactic outcomes in Chapter 3, the relevant judgement is not between a given system and a putatively perfect state of affairs defined as the complete absence of power relations, but can only ever be a *relative* one between different institutional arrangements. If this is accepted, then for Hayek private ownership is to be preferred, for whilst not wholly eradicating monopoly power, private property does minimize it relative to public ownership, because the monopoly power is a *de facto* rather than a legalized, or *de jure*, power. He does not need to claim, therefore, that under a liberal system permissive of private ownership there would be no relationships of power or *de facto* control by some of the means to the realization of the ends of others. Rather, all he needs to claim is that under public ownership these problems would not only be exacerbated but, as the results of a legally enforced monopoly, even harder to overcome.[31]

Hayek's epistemological arguments for individual liberty and the protection of individual domains have significant implications for his conception of the ideal role of the state which return us to the central theme of the cultivation rather than direction of the social process. Here the state's role should not be 'to determine particular results for particular individuals or groups' but only 'to provide certain generic conditions whose effects on the several individuals will be unpredictable'.[32] In a particularly interesting analogy, Hayek claims in *Rules and Order* that the function of government

> is somewhat like that of a maintenance squad of a factory, its object being not to produce any particular services or products to be consumed by the citizens, but rather to see that the mechanism which regulates the production of those goods and services is kept in working order. The purposes for which this machinery is currently being used will be determined by those who operate its parts and in the last resort by those who buy its products.[33]

Conservatism and libertarianism

Of course, Hayek's liberalism is not only open to the objections that it is overly economic in its concerns and that it not only ignores but positively encourages the use of coercive private power. Another possible objection to his theory of justice is that, despite his professed commitment to individual liberty, he is ultimately no liberal at all. Especially in view of the deep and central emphasis he places upon the importance of tradition and the limited nature of our powers of reason, it would be more appropriate to consider Hayek as a conservative. Yet, it seems that such a reading would be an inappropriate one and not simply because Hayek explicitly rejected it in the Postscript to *The Constitution of Liberty*.[34]

Central here are two considerations: the role of customary rules of just conduct, or tradition, in his political theory and his stance towards markets. With respect to the role of tradition there are at least two reasons why we should not view Hayek as a conservative. In the first instance, and as we saw in Chapter 2, tradition plays an instrumental rather than essential or constitutive role in his social theory. As Kenneth Minogue has noted this is because, unlike Hayek's account, the conservative defence of inherited traditions arises from 'a concern with our own concrete identity'. 'The conservative view,' it is stressed, 'is that we ought not lightly to challenge religious, or patriotic, or habitual practices and loyalties, because these things reveal to us what we are, and no politics that ignores what we are, in all our historical concreteness, can be successful'. This is in sharp contrast to Hayek's emphasis upon tradition that is 'based upon their consequences in promoting prosperity'.[35] To be sure, Hayek does at times come very close to endorsing tradition in conservative terms, although his discussion suggests an understanding of prosperity that is wider than the one Minogue ascribes to him.[36] For Hayek, we could say, traditions are instrumentally useful because they promote 'epistemic' rather than merely material prosperity. That is, they promote the maximization of that practical wisdom in terms of which we make our way in a complex social order which we can never know in any comprehensive fashion.[37] Moreover, this is not to say that in invoking tradition as a coordination device Hayek is not fundamentally concerned with identity. Rules, traditions and practices *are* intimately tied to our 'concrete identities' for, as we have seen, they not only serve to coordinate our action and provide an account of how we can successfully interpret one another's actions. In doing so they also constitute us insofar as they help to shape what actions we will actually take and which preferences we will form.[38] Despite this, however, and just because his defence of tradition is instrumental in nature rather than constitutive, it is not to be valued as a good in itself and as such worth preserving via state action as conservatives would have us believe.

Moreover, and with regard to the evaluative stance we ought to adopt towards them, it is clear that Hayek does not believe that rules, traditions and practices should be beyond our critical reach. Similar to the instrumental value of tradition as the foundation of social coordination, the reason for this also relates to Hayek's social theory. More specifically, and just as he claimed in his theory of mind that we cannot give an exhaustive explanation of all the rules of perception and action, so we cannot subject all the cultural rules we observe in our social lives to critical evaluation. '[W]e do not maintain,' he writes in *The Mirage of Social Justice*

that all tradition as such is sacred and exempt from criticism, but merely that the basis of criticism of any one product of tradition must always be other products of tradition which we either cannot or do not want to question; in other words, that particular aspects of a culture can be critically examined only within the context of that culture.[39]

In 'The Errors of Constructivism' he is even more explicit with respect to his attitude towards tradition where he says, within the context of an argument about the limits imposed upon the possibility of social criticism by our participation in tradition, that 'the conservatives among you, who up to this point may be rejoicing, will probably now be disappointed'. 'The proper conclusion from the considerations I have advanced', he adds,

> is by no means that we may confidently accept all the old traditional values. Nor even that there are *any* values or moral principles, which science may not occasionally question. The social scientist who endeavours to understand how society functions, and to discover where it can be improved, must claim the right critically to examine, and even to judge, every single value in our society. The consequence of what I have said is merely that we can never at one and the same time question *all* its values.[40]

Hayek's position, then, can be taken to occupy a midpoint between conservatism and a more radically critical perspective. Like the radical perspective, he does agree that criticism of potentially all the inherited rules, traditions and practices that govern our action is to be welcomed. At the same time, though, and in deference to the conservative position, such criticism can never be of the entire body of rules at once.[41] In addition to his non-reverential attitude towards tradition, Hayek's robust defence of markets gives a second reason that mitigates labelling him as a conservative. Indeed, to consider Hayek a conservative in this regard would be to run counter to a whole tradition of thought that, in the modern era, goes back at least as far as the writings of eighteenth-century thinker Justus Moser, who viewed markets with deep suspicion because of the threat they were taken to pose to cultural particularity.[42]

The issue of markets, not to mention the curious absence of any thoroughgoing or extended discussion of the importance of the value of equality to his project, moreover, opens up the possibility that Hayek is not properly liberal in another sense. Indeed, when these aspects of his thought are considered, it would be tempting to consider Hayek to be a libertarian who shares far more in common with a thinker such as Robert Nozick than he does with a liberal such as John Rawls.[43] Deciding whether Hayek is a libertarian will depend on whether one thinks of his work in terms of the policies and normative stances he adopts, or in terms of the philosophical stance he adopts when defending them. Thus, the similarity of their political recommendations notwithstanding, it would be an error to regard Hayek as a libertarian in the philosophical sense because of the nature of the foundation upon which he constructs his account of political association. As we have seen, Hayek's is an epistemological liberal justice in which individual rights are not the starting point of his project, as they are, for example, in the case of Nozick and, before him, John Locke, but are derived from his prior epistemological account of mind and the limits of reason.[44] The obvious similarities between their political commitments notwithstanding, it would be wrong to consider Hayek's theory to be libertarian in this strict philosophical sense, regardless of any similarities between their accounts of political association. Nevertheless, and even if only as a matter of emphasis rather than omission, the absence of a thoroughgoing discussion of the importance of equality to his project means that, for the time being at least, we have no particularly strong reason to consider Hayek to be a true exponent of liberal political theory for which the values of individual freedom and equality have always been central. In order to address this concern, and to complete our account of Hayek's normative enterprise, we need now to examine his legal theory.

Legal Theory

Defining individual domains

Hayek accepts that any adequate account of liberal justice must achieve more than the formal prioritization of individual freedom and the protection of individual domains. It also must give some specific content to these commitments.[45] The reason for this relates to the issue raised at the end of Chapter 2 about the occasional failure of the rules of just conduct to be honoured in action. We saw then that it is at this point that Hayek introduces the idea of the state, 'the embodiment of deliberately organized and consciously directed power', that is indispensable to the functioning of the spontaneous order of society and whose aim is 'to enforce a set of rules given to it, [which] requires the maintenance of an apparatus of courts, police, penal institutions, etc., and the application of particular means to particular purposes'.[46] Importantly, and precisely because the state is charged with securing the integrity of the rules of just conduct, an important part of its task is to articulate what those rules are. Because of this need for articulation, Hayek therefore needs to provide an account of law that makes institutionally concrete his epistemological argument for individual domains and he does so in two steps. The first step is Hayek's recognition that, consistent with his general epistemological perspective central to our understanding of the purpose of law is the Knowledge Problem. Any examination of the moral or legal order that leaves out the fact of our constitutional ignorance, he claims in *The Mirage of Social Justice*, 'misses the central problem' that law is supposed to address.[47] That is, just as defenders of central planning ignore the economic Knowledge Problem of deciding what to do with resources, the assumption of omniscience misses what we may call the 'legal knowledge problem' facing society.

Similarly to his social theory and his economics then, Hayek offers an account of law that enables individuals to adjust themselves, under conditions of limited knowledge, to ever-changing circumstances and it is in this sense that the law constitutes 'an adaptation of the whole of society to its environment'.[48] In *The Political Ideal of the Rule of Law* Hayek returns to one of his favourite themes concerning the ubiquity of complex phenomena in both the natural and social worlds and argues that we can learn a lot about the task of specifying the laws suitable to a regime of individual liberty by looking at the example of science. In the natural world, as we have seen, we often cannot have knowledge of the particular facts that bring about complex orders but rather only of the general laws of behaviour that govern their emergence. Despite this, we can 'employ our knowledge of such laws to bring about an organization of matter which we could not possibly produce by individually placing each particle just where we want it'. Importantly, Hayek also wants to emphasize that for such an order to emerge it is not necessary that some exogenous force be deliberately applied. '[I]f a multitude of individual elements obey certain general laws, 'he writes,' this may of course produce a definite order of the whole mass without the interference of an outside force.'[49] Equally significantly, however, our ability to make use of our knowledge of the laws that allow for the mutual adjustment necessary for the emergence of complex order also comes at a cost. '[T]his reliance on the spontaneous forces, which is our only means to achieve this result', he tells us, 'also means that we cannot control certain aspects of the process. We could, e.g., not at the same time rely on those forces and make sure that particular individual molecules will occupy particular places in the resulting structure'.[50]

Most significantly for Hayek, our ability to recognize that certain kinds of rule foster the mutual adjustment of a multiplicity of separate

elements without outside interference applies 'to the laws obeyed by
men no less than to the laws of nature' and 'is precisely the problem in
creating an order in society'.[51] This idea of law fostering mutual adjustment is important because it makes possible the second step in Hayek's
response to the concern about the absence of a convincing account of
the boundaries of individual domains. Central here is his claim that in
an important respect the concern motivating this kind of objection to
his legal theory overlooks Hayek's own concern to allow individuals *to
define their own private domains*. That is, and in opposition to the idea
that the appropriate philosophical task is to give a 'once-and-for-all'
account of individual domains, Hayek does not believe that it is desirable 'to have the particular contents of a man's private sphere fixed
once and for all'. In a complex society to do so would impinge upon
any future chance he may have to make the best use of and hence
contribute his own knowledge to the wider social process and would
run counter to the evolving nature of morality itself within whose context debates concerning the proper sphere of individual action take
place. For this reason Hayek claims that it is desirable for individuals
'*themselves* [to] have some voice in the determination of what will be
included in their personal protected sphere'. Indeed, he argues, if the
determination of this sphere were a matter of the 'deliberate assign-
ment of particular things to particular men', that is '[i]f what was to be
included in a man's private sphere were to be determined by the will
of any man of group of men, this would simply transfer the power of
coercion to that will'.[52]

The rule of law

The way individuals have a say in defining their own domains is not
only via philosophical reflection, for example about what would constitute a definitive list of enforceable individual rights and protections.
It may also occur via the recognition of general principles, not directly
governing the definition of the individual domain itself, but governing
the *rules* that define the conditions under which domains are defined.
Such principles would be pertinent in this way not only to the question
of the basis upon which material objects (or 'property') come legiti-
mately to belong to somebody's domain. The principles also do this
with regard to personal circumstances and what occurs within them
(what Hayek calls 'permissible actions') that are part of one's protected

sphere.[53] The general principles that determine what may count as law and thus which constitute his answer to the question of the demarcation of an individual's protected sphere is Hayek's conception of the rule of law and it is this account which we will now examine.

Before proceeding to examine Hayek's account of the rule of law, however, it is important to note the relationship of the *nomos* of Hayek's political and legal theory to the customary rules of just conduct in his social theory. In many respects, of course, these rules are very similar to one another, not least in their form. Importantly, however, they differ with respect to their function in Hayek's legal theory and this relates not only to his account of the cultivating rather than directing role of the state, but also to the role of *reason* in determining that role. More specifically, we will recall that in Hayek's social theory, the customary rules of just conduct are honoured in action and embody traditional and tacit knowledge. It is in this sense, moreover, that we either cannot or do not need to articulate them in order for them to serve their essential co-coordinating function. Matters are quite different, however, with regard to the customary rules of just conduct when they need to be enforced by the state as what Hayek calls *nomos*.[54] Firstly, and as we have seen, the very fact that the rules need to be legally enforced shows that they are not always honoured in action and it is for this reason that Hayek claims there needs to be a special organization, the state, whose specific aim is to enforce them when necessary. Secondly, and most importantly, the fact that they are enforced as *nomos* means that they need to be capable of articulation. In other words, in order to fulfil this aspect of its cultivating role, the state, or officers of the state, have to be able to explicitly declare what the law actually is, or what at least counts as a law worthy of legal enforcement. It is this question of what counts as law that Hayek addresses in his theory of the rule of law.

The concept of the rule of law is a notoriously nebulous one that has been subject to many and often conflicting understandings.[55] Nevertheless, one of the central ideas of the rule of law is that of the law being supreme and to which all are in some sense bound. Importantly for Hayek, however, the idea of the rule of law should not just be taken to include this well-known principle. The idea only includes traditional formulations, such as that of the government being 'a government of laws and not of men' that was incorporated into the *Constitution of Massachusetts* or, as Scottish theologian Samuel Rutherford put it almost 150 years before, that 'the law is king', not 'the king is the

law'.[56] Of equal importance, and to provide the grounding necessary
to adequately specify the process in which individuals define their own
domains, Hayek's theory additionally implies a set of principles, or a
'a meta-legal doctrine or a political ideal', that determine what legiti-
mately *counts* as law.[57]

From the various texts in which he discusses the rule of law, it is
clear that Hayek applies his understanding of the characteristics of
the customary rules of just conduct to his account of law, or *nomos*. He
cites six criteria for determining what should count as a law worthy of
enforcement by the state. Three are characteristics of the law itself,
three concern how the it should be applied. The first three criteria
are that *nomos* ought to be: general (or abstract), negative, and that it
satisfy the demands of equality. Moreover, it should be applied so that
it is known and certain, intended for the long term and be prospective or forward looking, rather than retrospective.[58] By being general
or abstract Hayek means that *nomos* is devoid of reference to specific
individuals or groups. Importantly, and to attest to the fundamentally epistemological orientation of Hayek's liberal jurisprudence, we
will also see that the underlying motivation for each criterion is its
serviceability to the coordination of the plans and utilisation of the
knowledge of disparate individuals acting under conditions of spatio-
temporal distancing in a complex society. In keeping with the epistemological timbre of his perspective, and as was the case with the
customary rules of just conduct, it is the abstractness and generality
of *nomos*, which allows it to serve its coordinating function by helping 'people to predict the behaviour of those with whom they must
collaborate'.[59] Later Hayek was to take inspiration from Kant and
reformulate the requirement of generality and abstractness to one
of a rule of just conduct's being capable of *universalization*. 'The test
of the justice of a rule', he writes, 'is usually (since Kant) described
as that of its "universalizability"; i.e. of the possibility of willing that
the rules should be applied to all instances that correspond to the
conditions stated in it (the "categorical imperative")'.[60] Hayek goes
on to say that the universalization test ultimately amounts to a test of
the compatibility of the rule under consideration with the wider body
of rules operative in the society concerned. Moreover, and again in
keeping with Hayek's fundamental epistemological concerns, this test
serves an important coordinative function in ensuring that the whole
body of rules is capable of giving definite guidance. The importance
of this, of course, is that without it, we would not be able to have

reasonable expectations about one another's behaviour and thus coordinate our plans with those of our fellows, the vast majority of whom remain unknown to us in a complex or 'Great' society. As he explains in *The Mirage of Social Justice*,

> the test of 'universalizability' applied to any one rule will amount to a test of compatibility with the whole system of accepted rules – a test which, as we have seen, may either lead to a clear 'yes' or 'no' answer or may show that, if the system of rules is to give definite guidance, some of the rules will have to be modified, or so arranged into a hierarchy of greater or lesser importance (or superiority or inferiority), that in the case of conflict we know which is to prevail and which is to give.[61]

We will see later on how the universalization test not only serves this coordinating function but also clarifies the appropriate *critical stance* we need to take towards the system of rules. For now we may note that, in a manner similar to the position Hayek adopted towards our ethical assessment of customary rules, the universalization test reflects the fact that

> [i]t is impossible to decide about the justice of any one particular rule of just conduct except within the framework of a whole system of such rules, most of which must for this purpose be regarded as unquestioned: values can always be tested only in terms of other values.[62]

Similar to his account of customary rules Hayek also claims that the rules of justice are negative in the sense of being prohibitions upon action rather than commands to undertake specific actions.[63] Moreover, it is, this aspect which also enables *nomos* to facilitate social coordination. Because it is based upon rules formulated as prohibitions rather than as commands, *nomos* allows individuals and organized groups to act upon and thus make use of their knowledge, rather than enjoin them to do a particular thing regardless of what they know.

Closely connected to its generality is the third characteristic Hayek attributes to *nomos:* that it satisfy the value of equality, or what he called, its *isonomy*.[64] Equality is important to Hayek in two respects. Firstly, equality is central insofar as he endorses the classical precept of the law not only applying equally to those subject to it, but that it is law for both the government and the governed. For Hayek, then, nobody is to be above the law.[65] Secondly, *nomos's* satisfying the value of equality is an extension of the idea of its generality and abstractness. That is, a rule of justice must be sufficiently general so as to be equally applicable to all within the jurisdiction.[66] Of course, being aware of a common objection to this criterion, Hayek accepts that even general rules can be formulated to pick out specific individuals or groups, and cites an amusing example given by his fellow participant in Mises' *Privatseminar* in Vienna, Gottfried Haberler to illustrate this. Haberler describes Germany's customs tariff of 1902 which, to avoid a most-favoured-nation obligation, was formulated so as to impose a special rate of import duty upon 'brown or dappled cows reared at a level of at least 300 meters above the sea and passing at least one month in every summer at a height of at least 800 meters'.[67] Perhaps as a means of warding off this danger, Hayek offers two additional criteria to bolster his commitment to equality before the law. First, in the event that a law does pick out a particular group, Hayek claims that a majority of those inside the group as well as a majority of those outside of it need to accept the law in order for it to be lawful.[68] Secondly, and perhaps most significantly, for Hayek it is not only a question of the law being formulated in general and abstract terms, or whether those affected by it accept it, but also that it must be general in its *effects*. If, despite a general formulation, the *operation* of the law were to result in the singling out of some individuals and groups, it would on this basis be inadmissible as *nomos*.

Hayek's account of equality is also significant because it provides an answer to the question posed earlier about whether his political theory should be considered liberal. It is clear that once his theory of the rule of law is taken into consideration, his political theory is quite clearly liberal in character. This is obscured in his economic and political theory because Hayek is at pains to emphasize the value of individual liberty in order to provide a convincing response to the Knowledge Problem. This response notwithstanding, there is another objection to Hayek's account of equality. Despite the textual evidence available for rejecting the charge that he has no account of equality, we may nonetheless criticize Hayek for not attending sufficiently to the value of its enjoyment, even from within the context of what some would claim is his already-diminished formal commitment. Illustrative of Hayek's problem here is that, even with respect to formal equality, it is still very possible, especially for members of historically less powerful or marginal minority groups, to be the victims of social processes – for example, a culture of indifference in the police force or judiciary – that undermines their enjoyment of the formal rights and freedoms that they are supposed to enjoy equally with others. Thus, whilst not being vulnerable to the charge that his theory would permit, for example, the legal establishment of couverture, Hayek is nonetheless insensitive to the ways in which women and other traditionally less powerful groups, may not enjoy their basic rights and freedoms as much as others, even where a constitution says that, on paper, they should. The implication of this objection, of course, is that even the Hayekian cultivating state may need, in the interests of not substantive equality, but of the equal enjoyment of formal equality, to take considerable and quite possibly intrusive steps to make good on its role.

Before concluding the outline of the theory of the rule of law, we need to note the three criteria that relate to the application of *nomos*. In each case, and consistent with his underlying perspective, Hayek offers a coordination argument for this characteristic, claiming that without them we would not be able to properly plan under complex social conditions. First, and given their prospective rather than retrospective character, the rules of justice apply to an unknown number of future instances.[69] In addition they are to be known and certain. Indeed, he claims, that the measure to which the law is certain is shown by the number of disputes that never reach court because the outcome is known in advance by both sides.[70] Finally, *nomos* operates over the long term, although it is subject to revision in the light of changing circumstances.[71]

The common law as a legal discovery procedure

Having set out the six criteria for sound law that inform its articulation as *nomos*, Hayek also needs to offer an account of how this is actually done. He specifies a number of mechanisms for this, the most important of which is that of the role of the judge in a specifically common law legal system. Hayek's attachment to the common law and the role he understands the judge to play in it is intimately related to the underlying epistemological concern of his political and legal theory. The judge, of course, is concerned with deciding which among the expectations of disputing parties have been illegitimately disappointed by the violation of a rule of just conduct. Moreover, in cases that are not relevantly similar to any previous case, the judge articulates the law with reference to the cultural norms already implicit in the community.[72] In performing both tasks, the judge serves a social and coordinative function: he not only resolves the case at hand but, in doing so, signals to the entire jurisdiction which expectations are legitimate.

Of course, in large-scale societies there is never just one but, rather, numerous judges who continually decide cases. This is significant because it points to the fact that for Hayek the development of the common law is in an important sense also spontaneous and is in effect his second discovery procedure. However, rather than being an economic discovery procedure, the gradual evolution of the common law represents a legal or juridical procedure that enables society to determine which norms ought to be honoured. To be sure, the specific aggregate of laws that emerges out of the decisions of judges is, like the order it helps to sustain, not a part of any one of those judges' intentions; each is only concerned with the resolution of the particular dispute before him. Out of each decision, nevertheless, the content of the law gradually adjusts itself to ever-changing circumstances, whilst remaining internally consistent and providing the legal basis for legitimate expectations and social coordination.[73] The six criteria of *nomos*, then, can be interpreted as being held in the mind of the *judge* when applying laws already established as precedent, or else when coming to articulate laws that are already honoured in action in the case of judgments about new circumstances. The legal theory that Hayek offers, then, is not a once-and-for-all philosophical account of the proper limits of individual domains. Rather, he offers a procedure by which we may seek to discover what those limits are via our own efforts and, when these lead us into conflict with one another, via the common law and the person of the judge.

One may object here that investing such authority in judges will give them free reign in the determination of individual fates. Moreover, narrow self-interest will perhaps further distort the legal process as judges seek to impose adjudications that are consonant with their own, unadmitted, interests rather than with the establishment of legitimate expectations.[74] Consequently, it is to the democratic appointment of judges that we must look so that they will be directly beholden to the public on whose behalf they are supposed to deliver justice. This objection, however, is unpersuasive on at least four counts. Firstly, it

ignores the central value of equality as expressed in the idea that like
cases must be treated alike and how this relates to the authority of
precedent in the common law process. What precedent achieves, of
course, is to delimit in advance the kinds of adjudication that judges
can make, given the particular cases before them. Indeed, that is what
is meant by judges being 'bound' by precedent rather than being free
to decide cases in any manner they choose.[75] Moreover, it is unclear
how subjecting the appointment of judges to democratic procedures
would do much to address the problem of self-interest. Within a democratic setting a judge would be beholden to the promises he makes
in his election campaign – say a commitment to punish more child
killers – as well as the often short-term interests of an outraged public
with whom he now has an accountable relationship. It is not unreasonable, therefore, to claim that the election of judges would distort
the judicial process more gravely than does the system of unelected
judges. Third, where there is no precedent – that is, where the case
before a judge is novel – he nevertheless settles it with reference to the
pre-existing rules of just conduct already latent in society, rather than
according to his own proclivities. The same considerations apply even
more clearly in criminal cases involving trial by jury. Here it is the
defendant's *peers* who determine culpability with reference to the customary rules of just conduct that constitute the moral tradition of the
community.[76] Finally, Hayek points to the fact that the judge's decisions are in any case themselves subject to appeal in a higher court.[77]

The state and legislation, or *thesis*

Despite the central importance he attaches to the common law and
to common law judges, Hayek does accept the need for correction
of the common law by legislation.[78] First, there are occasions when
its gradual development runs into what he calls evolutionary dead-
ends from which it needs to be extricated. Secondly, it is possible that,
owing to sudden technological advance, the common law does not
evolve quickly enough. On both of these occasions, Hayek contends, it
is the role of the government to decide what the law should be and it
is here where legislators need to bear the principles of the rule of law
in mind. Hayek also recognizes, however, that there is no guarantee
that they will do this effectively.[79] It is for this reason that he claims
that the distinction between *nomos* and *thesis*, between law properly

understood, and legislation, does *not* correspond to that between customary and common law on the one hand and the statutes passed in
a legislature on the other. Indeed, it is because of the worry about the
potential failure of legislators to pass measures in conformity with the
rule of law, that Hayek is concerned to emphasize the intellectual possibility of the articulation of the *attributes* of *nomos*. This is important,
of course, because it creates the possibility of the legislature correcting defects in the common law when necessary.[80] By the same token,
and in view of his worry about the failings of legislators, decoupling
the attributes of law from its source also means that Hayek has the
grounds to claim that laws passed in a legislature do not automatically
merit being considered as law. This manoeuvre, we will see in the next
chapter, is crucial to his constitutional project of salvaging democracy
and containing the power of the state.

In addition to its function as occasional articulator of *nomos*, we have
seen that Hayek locates a role for the state in its duty to enforce it.
This duty is significant for his account of legislation because, as with
any organization that has a specific function, the state needs to have
rules of organization to properly carry it out. In contrast to the statutes
it passes that have the character of *nomos*, these special rules of organization Hayek calls *thesis*.[81] In contrast to the purpose independent,
abstract and negative character of *nomos*, *thesis* is defined in terms of
the administrative purpose it serves and is given in the form of commands. 'The law of organization of government', Hayek writes, 'is not
law in the sense of rules defining what kind of conduct is generally
right, but consists of directions concerning what particular officers or
agencies of government are required to do'.[82] Among the examples of
thesis Hayek notes constitutional law, financial legislation, administrative law and law governing police power and the courts.

The Adequacy of Hayek's Political and Legal Theory

How persuasive is Hayek's account of the meta-legal criteria that
he claims restrict what one may classify as *nomos*, in the name of
the protection of individual domains? Chandran Kukathas and
Richard Bellamy claim that it is not clear whether the criteria Hayek
provides actually rule out many of the rules of justice that he and
liberals more generally would want ruled out.[83] More specifically,

for Kukathas, the absence of a convincing moral theory to ground Hayek's account of the rule of law means that the criteria he does offer do not properly set out the limits of one's protected domain. This is because some laws which liberals would consider unjust – such as those pertaining to religious conformity and, we may add, to family relations and the status of homosexuals – may be quite general and yet be uniquely felt as onerous by some groups. Citing the example of homosexuality in *The Constitution of Liberty*, Hayek attempts to resolve this problem by claiming that the very private nature of such relations means that such laws do not limit conduct towards others and, as such cannot be acceptable as rules of justice.[84] The judge, he tells us elsewhere, is only concerned with the effects of individual action upon others and not with 'private' behaviour where one only affects oneself or others on a voluntary basis.[85] Yet, Kukathas contends, Hayek's response presupposes that we are clear as to what constitutes affecting others. We may, for example, be annoyed by the fact that somebody practices a religion or has sexual preferences different to our own and claim that their behaviour affects us adversely. Having found Hayek's account of law wanting, Kukathas investigates whether any other aspect of his political theory may give substance to the account of individual domains and concludes that it cannot. It is unclear, he notes, whether Hayek is capable of offering '*any* moral theory which would enable us to specify the kinds of rules of entitlement, or identify the rights, which should characterise the liberal order'.[86]

To be fair to Hayek, and as Roland Kley has pointed out, even Kukathas accepts that 'moral justification was not Hayek's chief aim'.[87] To judge the adequacy of his political project in these terms, then, may be to misjudge them. Rather than examine his ethical arguments for liberal individualism, Kley suggests that it is to the instrumental nature of Hayek's claims that attention must be paid when assessing the overall persuasiveness of his theory. Such an interpretation is provided by Kley, one of whose central arguments is that, for Hayek himself, it is because of the *efficiency* of markets and liberal individualist institutions in general at utilizing social knowledge, and not because they are the institutionalization of an ethical commitment to individual liberty *per se*, that liberalism is to be recommended. Such a reading, however, presents its own problems for Hayek. Precisely because of its amoral, instrumental nature, Hayek's theory is ultimately insufficient as a defence of classical liberalism. 'Markets must, as [Hayek] rightly insists', Kley writes, 'play an important role. Yet how far they should extend, how far they should be constrained and in what ways supplemented, and in what kind of political framework they should be embedded, cannot be decided on grounds of feasibility alone'.[88] Similarly, and whilst conceding that Hayek's arguments deliver a devastating blow to 'the most hubristic types of economic planning', John Gray claims that they contain little if anything to aid us in choosing between different ways of organizing the market.[89] Answering such questions is not something that Hayek can help us with because it 'requires genuine *moral* reflection and falls in *the province of normative political philosophy*'.[90] The moral dimension is precisely what Hayek's theory needs – and lacks.

It is, however, precisely in Hayek's epistemological argumentation that a response to this important objection may be found. Here, it is possible to read Hayek as defending his conception of law as, on amoral, *epistemological* grounds, the answer to the Knowledge Problem that characterizes our discovery of an answer to the question of how far individual domains and the free markets their legal protection makes possible should extend. Thus, even if we concede the line of objection of the thinkers above, the question then arises as to *who* is to decide upon the ethical values that are to determine the scope and extent of private domains. More specifically and precisely because of the universality of the Knowledge Problem that Hayek's account of mind and society presents, it seems difficult to provide an adequate answer to this question without assuming the constructivist attitude Hayek gives us reason to reject. If, that is, the regime of individual liberty is to be preferred to politics because of the relative epistemological advantages it confers, then we would need to hear why, with respect to coordinating our moral knowledge about how far private domains and the proprietary arrangements they make possible should extend, it would not be able to do so.

On this reading, the objection that Hayek's theory lacks an adequate moral foundation appears to rest on a misreading of his project. It is not the case that his theory of justice betrays a lack of genuine moral reflection in the process of defining the proper scope of individual domains. Rather, it points to the deeper question of on what institutional basis the defining should take place. All it says is that for epistemological reasons, such reflection should not take place only within politics or within the mind of the political philosopher, but rather within the cultural and the legal process. Similar to the constructivist account of social order that Hayek gives us reason to reject, Kley's critique mistakenly assumes that moral values remain in some asocial autonomous domain and do not emerge out of the same kind of social interaction that yields prices or other kinds of information. Ultimately, Kley's reading overlooks the fact that Hayek's theory rests on an amoral, but nonetheless universal, claim about human reason which issues in a normative argument for a particular institutional framework that maximizes, relative to other known institutions, the emergence, coordination and use of economic and *moral* knowledge in a complex society. Thus, if we appeal to other considerations to determine the scope of individual domains, we still need liberal individual rights to elicit the content of these considerations as fully as possible.

Most serious however is a second objection that, despite the amoral, epistemological basis of his liberalism, Hayek claims that the notion of the rule of law forms part 'of the *moral* tradition of the community, a common ideal shared and unquestioningly accepted by the majority'.[91] Problematically, however, we may reasonably claim that this runs counter to his theory of cultural evolution. The question here is what happens if our moral tradition evolves *away* from the view that privileges individual liberty? Indeed, this is a possibility that Hayek is clearly aware of as he spends considerable time giving an historical account of the development and ultimately decline of the idea of the rule of law.[92] Of course, Hayek could abandon this option and ground the public acceptance of the ideal solely upon epistemological considerations. But doing this leads to an additional problem that suggests a wider issue concerning the persuasiveness of his liberalism. Given that at the foundation of Hayek's theory is not an ethical claim about the ends of life, our status as moral beings, or of our most essential interests, but rather an amoral epistemological claim concerning the nature of knowledge and reason in a complex society, his epistemological liberalism may, whilst guaranteeing neutrality simply because it makes no appeal to the ethical at all, rest on decidedly shaky foundations. For if one vacates the terrain of ethical justification altogether as Hayek clearly does, the result would seem to be an account of justice that is *theoretically* endorseable by all, but actually endorsed by *no-one* for want of sufficient moral motivation.

Notes

[1] Hayek, 'Kinds of Rationalism', in Hayek, F.A. (ed.), *Studies in Philosophy, Politics and Economics*, London, Routledge and Kegan Paul, (1965) 1967, p. 91.

[2] Ibid., p. 92.

[3] Ibid.

[4] Hayek, 'TheUse of Knowledge in Society', in Hayek, F.A. (ed.), *Individualism and Economic Order*, Chicago, IL, University of Chicago Press, (1945) 1948, p. 88.

[5] Hayek, 'Kinds of Rationalism', p. 91.

[6] Hayek, *Rules and Order*, London, Routledge, 1973, p. 13.

[7] Hayek, *Rules and Order*, pp. 12–13. See also Hayek, *The Political Ideal of the Rule of Law*, Cairo, National Bank of Egypt, 1955a, p. 31.

[8] Hayek, *The Mirage of Social Justice*, London, Routledge, 1976a, p. 8.

[9] Hayek, *Rules and Order*, p. 13.

[10] Hayek, *The Mirage of Social Justice*, p. 39.

[11] Hume, D., *Enquiry Concerning the Principles of Morals*, Oxford, Oxford University Press, (1751) 1995, §III, Part I, esp. p.188. See also Hume, D., *A Treatise of Human Nature*, Oxford, Oxford University Press, (1740) 1978, Book II, Part II, §II, esp. pp. 486–489, 494.

[12] Rawls, J., *A Theory of Justice*, Oxford, Oxford University Press, 1971, pp.126–130.

[13] Hayek, *Rules and Order*, p.13, emphasis added.

[14] Hayek, *The Mirage of Social Justice*, p. 83.

[15] Hume, A Treatise of Human Nature, p. 487.

[16] Hayek, 'Individualism: True and False', in Hayek, F. A. (ed.), *Individualism and Economic Order*, Chicago, IL, University of Chicago Press, (1946a) 1948, p. 6.

[17] Hayek, *The Constitution of Liberty*, London, Routledge, 1960, pp. 29–30; 'The Principles of a Liberal Social Order', (1966), *Studies in Philosophy, Politics and Economics*, London, Routledge and Kegan Paul, 1967, pp. 160–177; 'Liberalism' (1973c), *New Studies in Philosophy, Politics, Economics and the History of Ideas*, London, Routledge and Kegan Paul, 1978, pp. 119–151; *Rules and Order*, pp. 57, 61.

[18] Hayek, *The Political Ideal of the Rule of Law*, pp. 31–32, 43–45. To be sure, Hayek does accept circumstances – for example in the event of natural disasters – that allow for that sphere to be overriden. See *The Political Ideal of the Rule of Law*, pp. 44.

[19] Hayek, *The Mirage of Social Justice*, p. 37. See also Hayek, *The Constitution of Liberty*, p. 140.

[20] Hayek, F. A., 'The Moral Element in Free Enterprise', in Hayek, F. A. (ed.), *Studies in Philosophy, Politics and Economics*, London, Routledge and Kegan Paul, (1962b) 1967, p. 233.

[21] Hayek, *The Constitution of Liberty*, p. 29. See also Hayek, 'Individualism: True and False', pp. 10–11; *Rules and Order*, pp. 106–110, 115–118; *The Mirage of Social Justice*, p. 9; 'The Principles of a Liberal Social Order', p. 162.

22 Mill, J. S., *On Liberty*, Cambridge, Cambridge University Ptess, (1859) 2005, chapter 2.
23 Hayek, *The Constitution of Liberty*, pp. 32–35, 110, emphasis added. See also Hayek,'The Meaning of Competition', p. 106; 'Liberalism', pp. 147–149.
24 Hayek, *The Constitution of Liberty*, p. 35, emphasis added.
25 Hayek, *The Constitution of Liberty*, p. 33. See also Hayek, 'Liberalism', p. 149; *The Mirage of Social Justice*, pp. 8–9.
26 Hayek, *The Mirage of Social Justice*, pp. 8–11; *The Constitution of Liberty*, pp. 30–31.
27 Hayek, *The Constitution of Liberty*, p. 35, emphasis added.
28 Hayek, 'Liberalism', p. 149. See also Hayek, *The Road to Serfdom*, Chicago, IL, University of Chicago Press, (1944) 1976, p. 92.
29 Ibid., p. 149.
30 For a standard account of this argument see Daniel, N., 'Equal Liberty and Unequal Worth of Liberty', in Daniel, N. (ed.), *Reading Rawls: Critical Studies of 'A Theory of Justice'*, New York, Basic Books, 1975, pp. 253–281. See also Rawls, *A Theory of Justice*, p. 204; *Political Liberalism, Political Liberalism*, Columbia, NY, Columbia University Press, 1993, pp. 324–331.
31 Hayek, *The Constitution of Liberty*, p. 137; *The Political Order of a Free People*, London, Routledge, 1979, pp. 77–89.
32 Hayek, *The Mirage of Social Justice*, pp. 8, 2. See also 'Individualism: True and False', p. 16, emphasis added; *The Constitution of Liberty*, pp. 29–38.
33 Hayek, *Rules and Order*, p. 47. See also Hayek, *The Political Ideal of the Rule of Law*, p. 31; 'The Pretence of Knowledge', p. 34.
34 Hayek, *The Constitution of Liberty*, pp. 397–411.
35 Minogue, K., 'Hayek and Conservatism: Beatrice and Benedick?', in Butler, E. and Pirie, M. (eds), *Hayek on the Fabric of Human Society*, London, Adam Smith Institute, 1987, pp. 127–145.
36 Hayek, 'The Errors of Constructivism', in Hayek, F. A. (ed.), *New Studies in Philosophy, Politics, Economics and the History of Ideas*, London, Routledge and Kegan Paul, (1970) 1978, p. 19.
37 Hayek, *The Constitution of Liberty*, pp. 62, 66–67.
38 Hayek, *The Constitution of Liberty*, p. 24; 'Kinds of Rationalism', pp. 87–88. See also Galeotti, A. E. 'Individualism, Social Rules, Tradition: The Case of Friedrich A. Hayek', *Political Theory*, vol. 15, no. 2, May 1987, pp. 163–181.
39 Hayek, *The Mirage of Social Justice*, p. 25.
40 Hayek 'The Errors of Constructivism', p. 19.
41 Ibid.
42 For a useful overview see Muller, J., *The Mind and the Market: Capitalism in Western Thought*, New York, Anchor Books, 2002, Chapter 4. See also Scruton, R., 'Hayek and conservatism', in Feser, E. (ed.) *The Cambridge Companion to Hayek*, Cambridge, Cambridge University Press, 2006, pp. 223–228.
43 See Nozick, R., *Anarchy, State and Utopia*, New York, Basic Books, 1974; Rawls, *Theory of Justice*.
44 See, Locke, *Two Treatises of Government*, Cambridge, Cambridge University Press, (1690) 2005.
45 Hayek, 'Individualism: True and False', p. 17; *The Constitution of Liberty*, p. 139; *Rules and Order*, pp. 108–109.

⁴⁶ Hayek, *The Political Order of a Free People*, p. 23. See also Hayek, 'Individualism: True and False', p. 22; *Rules and Order*, p.47.

⁴⁷ Hayek, *The Mirage of Social Justice*, p. 8. See also Hayek, *The Political Ideal of the Rule of Law*, p. 31.

⁴⁸ Hayek, *The Political Ideal of the Rule of Law*, p. 31. See also Hayek, *The Constitution of Liberty*, pp. 156–157, 48; *Rules and Order*, pp. 72–76; *The Mirage of Social Justice*, pp. 8–12.

⁴⁹ Hayek, *The Political Ideal of the Rule of Law*, p. 30.

⁵⁰ Ibid., p. 31.

⁵¹ Ibid., pp. 30–31, emphasis added.

⁵² Hayek, *The Constitution of Liberty*, pp. 139–140, emphasis added. See also *The Mirage of Social Justice*, pp. 35–37.

⁵³ Ibid., p. 140.

⁵⁴ Hayek, *Rules and Order*, pp. 94–123.

⁵⁵ Shklar, J. 'Political Theory and the Rule of Law', in Shklar, J. (ed.), *Political Thought and Political Thinkers*, Chicago, IL, University of Chicago Press, (1987) 1998, pp. 21–37.

⁵⁶ On this see Rutherford, S., *Lex, Rex*, Ashburn, Hess Publishing, (1644) 1998. See also Hayek, *The Constitution of Liberty*, pp. 169, 182. On a government of laws see *Constitution of Massachusetts*, Part I, article XXX (1780).

⁵⁷ Hayek, *The Constitution of Liberty*, pp. 206, 218; *The Political Ideal of the Rule of Law*, pp. 25–28, 32–34; 'The Principles of a Liberal Social order', p. 163; *Rules and Order*, pp. 112–113; *The Mirage of Social Justice*, pp. 1–5. As such Hayek's account occupies a similar place to the idea of the Original Position in Rawls's account of justice insofar as both are theories about what laws ought to be. On this, see Kukathas, *Hayek and Modern Liberalism*, Oxford, Clarendon Press, 1989, pp. 154–155; Rawls, *A Theory of Justice*, Chapter 1, §§ 3 & 4. It is on the basis of this understanding, moreover, that Kukathas is critical of Raz's assessment of Hayek's account of law. On this see Kukathas, *Hayek and Modern Liberalism*, p. 155; Raz, J., 'The Rule of Law and Its Virtues', in Raz, J. (ed.), *Law and Morality*, Oxford, Oxford University Press, 1983, pp. 210–232.

⁵⁸ Hayek, *The Political Ideal of the Rule of Law*, pp. 34–36; *The Constitution of Liberty*, pp. 148–150, 208–210; 'The Principles of a Liberal Social Order', pp. 166–168; *Rules and Order*, chapters 4 and 5; 'Liberalism', pp. 134–135; *The Mirage of Social Justice*, chapter 7.

⁵⁹ Hayek, *The Road to Serfdom*, p. 73. See also Hayek, *The Consitution of Liberty*, pp. 156–158.

⁶⁰ Hayek, 'The Principles of a Liberal Social Order', p. 168. See also Hayek, *The Mirage of Social Justice*, pp. 27–29.

⁶¹ Hayek, *The Mirage of Social Justice*, pp. 28–29. See also Hayek, 'The Principles of a Liberal Social Order', p. 168.

⁶² Hayek, 'The Principles of a Liberal Social Order', p. 168. See also Hayek, *The Mirage of Social Justice*, pp. 24–27.

⁶³ Hayek, *The Consitution of Liberty*, p. 152; *The Mirage of Social Justice*, pp. 35–38; 'The Principles of a Liberal Social Order', pp. 166–167.

⁶⁴ Hayek, *The Political Ideal of the Rule of Law*, pp. 6–9, 35–36; *The Road to Serfdom*, pp. 59, 79–80.

[65] Ibid., pp. 209–210.

[66] Hayek, *The Consitution of Liberty*, p. 209.

[67] Quoted in Ibid., p. 489, n. 19.

[68] Ibid., pp. 209–210.

[69] Ibid., p. 208.

[70] Hayek, *The Political Ideal of the Rule of Law*, p. 36; *The Consitution of Liberty*, pp. 208–209.

[71] Hayek, *The Mirage of Social Justice*, pp. 29–30; *Rules and Order*, p. 122; 'Economic Freedom and Representative Government', in Hayek, F. A. (ed.), *New Studies in Philosophy, Politics, Economics and the History of Ideas*, London, Routledge and Kegan Paul, (1973b) 1978, pp. 113–114.

[72] Hayek, *Rules and Order*, p. 118; *The Mirage of Social Justice*, pp. 24–27.

[73] See also Leoni, B., *Freedom and the Law*, Los Angeles, Nash Publishing, (1961) 1972, pp. 21–22 who develops this theme. See also Baumgarth, W. P. 'Hayek and Political Order: The Rule of Law', *Journal of Libertarian Studies*, vol. 2, no. 1, 1978, pp. 24–25.

[74] Hayek, *Rules and Order*, pp. 88–89.

[75] Ibid., pp. 98–110, 123.

[76] Ibid., pp. 96–97.

[77] Hayek, *The Consitution of Liberty*, p. 212.

[78] Hayek, *Rules and Order*, p. 89.

[79] Ibid., pp. 127–128.

[80] Ibid., p. 127.

[81] Ibid., pp. 124–144.

[82] Ibid., p. 133.

[83] On this see Kukathas, *Hayek and Modern Liberalism*, pp. 157–165; Bellamy, R., *Liberalism and Pluralism: Towards a Politics of Compromise*, London, Routledge, 1999, pp. 29–34.

[84] Hayek, *The Constitution of Liberty*, p. 451, n. 18.

[85] Hayek, *Rules and Order*, p. 101; *The Constitution of Liberty*, pp. 145–146.

[86] Kukathas, *Hayek and Modern Liberalism*, p. 167.

[87] Kley, *Hayek's Social and Political Thought*, Oxford, Clarendon Press, 1994, p.11, footnote 12.

[88] Ibid., pp. 228–229.

[89] Gray, *Hayek on Liberty*, London, Routledge, 3rd edn, (1984) 1998, pp. 150–155.

[90] Kley, op. cit., p. 229, emphasis added.

[91] Hayek, *The Constitution of Liberty*, p. 206. See also Hayek, *Rules and Order*, p. 61.

[92] Hayek, *The Constitution of Liberty*, pp. 162–204; *Rules and Order*, pp.81–85; Hayek, F. A., 'Decline of the Rule of Law – I', *The Freeman*, April 20, 1953, pp. 518–520; Hayek, F. A.'Decline of The Rule of Law – II', May 4, 1953, *The Freeman*, pp. 561–563.

5

Democracy and the Model Constitution

Democracy and the Rule of Law

Hayek's critique of modern liberal democracy

Despite the weakness of his account of justice, Hayek does have much of interest to say about the relationship between it, the rule of law and what he sees as the miscarriage of the democratic ideal in modern times. More specifically, he claims that our inability to accept catallactic outcomes as just – an inability which, we have seen, he claims is based upon a faulty epistemology – has led to a fundamental change in our views about the purpose of democratic government. This is a change, moreover, that has in turn proven prejudicial to both individual liberty, the rule of law and ultimately to the esteem in which democracy itself is held. Perhaps most significantly, Hayek's diagnosis of the problems attendant to modern liberal democracy leads him not only to conclusions about the state which some may find surprising, but serves as the basis for his suggested solution to them.

In keeping with his epistemological view that the state should not exceed its role as cultivator of the environment conducive to spontaneous order, at the core of Hayek's critique of modern democracy is the suggestion that the important distinction, between the idea of government as director and government as cultivator of complex order, has been blurred.[1] The explanation for this, he claims, is to be found in the failure of the doctrine of the separation of powers and in our misunderstanding of the proper limits of popular sovereignty. Historically, the separation of powers was the device which, it was hoped, would help secure individual liberty and avoid arbitrary government, especially arbitrary *monarchical* government, by imposing clear restrictions on what government could do, most obviously by sanctioning coercion only in the interest of the enforcement of the rules of justice.[2] These rules in turn were considered just only if they accorded with the settled,

pre-political general *opinion* of what was right and wrong, regardless of
the particular and often temporary interest, or what Hayek calls the
will, of the monarch. More specifically, Hayek notes that the authority
of the monarch as lawgiver rested on his capacity to prove the justice of
his pronouncements by 'committing himself to their universal application to an unknown number of future instances and renouncing the
power of modifying their application to particular cases'.[3] In this way,
the monarch's pronouncements upon matters of law would be seen
to accord with the generally held moral opinion of his subjects that
like cases be treated alike and not merely be the expression of his own
personal preferences or interests. This gradual constitutionalization of
monarchy, Hayek notes, was just one of a succession of developments
in which '[f]or centuries efforts had been directed towards limiting
the powers of government'.[4]

However, the advent of representative democracy and the idea of
popular sovereignty presented a new challenge. 'Suddenly', he continues, 'it was believed that the control of government by elected
representatives of the majority made other checks on the powers of
government unnecessary'.[5] How, after all, would it be possible for
the people, or their representatives, to govern arbitrarily when the
governors and the governed were now effectively one and the same?
Hayek, however, was not alone in thinking that this view was both mistaken and dangerous. Indeed, the problem he highlights is not an
especially new one, being in a significant respect a repetition of the
account of the changing nature of the conflict between liberty and
authority described by Alexis de Tocqueville in *Democracy in America*
and J. S. Mill in the opening passages of *On Liberty*.[6] Mill, of course,
contended that, after having secured its liberty against the arbitrary
will of the monarch, it was naïvely believed that 'the nation did not
need to be protected against its own will' because '[t]here was no fear
of its tyrannising over itself'.[7] Given, he adds, that 'all those restraints
upon the supreme power that had been painfully built up during the
evolution of constitutional monarchy were successively dismantled as
no longer necessary', the modern presumption has been for law to be
that which is passed in a democratic legislature.[8] Whereas previously
coercion was legitimate only if it were approved of according to the
opinion of the majority, with the modern misconception of popular
sovereignty, it now meant 'that *all* that the majority approves shall have
that force'.[9] Similar to the path taken by the evolution of the British
state, in Hayek's view, is that of the constitution of the United States.

Despite achieving a separation of powers between the executive, legislative and judicial branches, the framers failed to separate the task of directing government activity to specific ends from that of stating what the rules of just conduct were.[10]

The consequence of this state of affairs 'in which a majority of a representative body lays down the law *and* directs government' has been the replacement of the conception of government as limited to cultivating the environment conducive to complex order by one in which its powers are in principle unlimited.[11] Yet, there is considerable danger when these different *legislative* and *governmental* functions are performed by the same representative assembly, or by different representative assemblies composed in the same way. This is particularly evident, notes Hayek, again following Mill, with respect to minorities, for such a view is blind to the danger posed by majorities that pass laws inimical to the formers' interests, and *in extremis*, prejudicial to their physical well-being.[12] Thus, as Hayek concludes in *The Constitution of Liberty*, '[t]he ideal of democracy, originally intended to prevent all arbitrary power, thus becomes the justification for a new arbitrary power'.[13] It is for this reason, he contends, that

> the ultimate power of government was in no democratic country of modern times ever under the law, because it was always in the hands of a body free to make whatever law it wanted for the particular tasks it desired to undertake.[14]

Continuing, Hayek states that we need to remind ourselves

> of the error we committed by sweeping away all the safeguards by which we had learnt effectively to hedge about constitutional *monarchy* under the illusion that once the will of the people governed there was no longer any need for the majority to prove that it regarded as just what it decided.[15]

Because, therefore, it ultimately failed to distinguish between the function of stating what the rules of justice were and of running the day-to-day affairs of government, an effective separation of powers has never been achieved.[16] To be sure, Hayek does not wish to claim that the different branches of government responsible for what he thinks ought to be organizationally separate tasks should not themselves be organized democratically. Democratic legislation in which representatives of the people 'decide on the laying down of rules of just conduct' when everyday morality and the common law fail to do so, and democratic government in which like representatives decide 'on the current activities of government in providing services by means of the resources placed at its disposal', are *both* ideas which he supports and works into his constitutional theory.[17]

Special interest politics and the paradoxical weakness of the omnipotent democratic state

What in Hayek's view are the consequences for the rule of law of the abandonment of constitutionalism and the adoption of unlimited democracy? The first is the possibility of arbitrary government in the sense that majoritarian decision-making of this kind represents 'action determined by a particular will unrestrained by a general rule'.[18] At this stage of the analysis it is irrelevant whether this particular will is the unchecked will of a dictator, or, as Hayek discusses, a democratic majority. Significantly, the arbitrariness in question is not sourced in the *number* of people who will the measure, but rather in that measure's not conforming to the rule of law that holds independently of that will. '[T]he conception of the rule of law', as we saw in the previous chapter 'presupposes a concept of law defined by the *attributes of the rules*, not by their source'.[19] In modern democracy, however, no longer does a law count as such because of its formal properties and relationship to preponderant opinion about what is just, but rather merely because it is sourced in a democratic legislature.[20] It is for this reason that, perhaps contrary to expectations, modern democracy does not protect us from the danger of arbitrariness. '[I]t is not the source but the *limitation* of power', writes Hayek, 'that prevents it from being arbitrary'.[21]

A second consequence of unlimited democracy for Hayek is that of the increase in the power of what he calls 'organized interests'.[22] When the democratic chamber is able to direct government and decide what is just, it is only natural that coalitions of voters with identical interests will form in order to ensure the passage of laws favourable to themselves. In the vast majority of particular cases, each of these interests in such a 'bargaining democracy' is by itself quite weak and very rarely approaches a majority of the electorate. The only way that such particular interests can be satisfied, therefore, is by the groups who have them joining still larger coalitions with other interest groups so that together they do form an electoral majority. More specifically, Hayek notes, where there is 'a distribution of incomes chiefly determined by political power' there grows an apparatus of para-government consisting of trade associations, trades unions and professional organizations whose business it is to divert 'as much as possible of the stream of governmental favour to their members'.[23] Moreover, such an outcome is inevitable in an unlimited democratic regime because a government can only remain in power 'by satisfying a sufficiently large number of pressure groups to assure itself of the support of a majority'.[24] The government will then be forced, Hayek notes,

> to bring together and keep together a majority by satisfying the demands of a multitude of special interests, each of which will consent to the special interests granted to other groups only at the price of their own special interests being equally considered.[25]

Importantly, Hayek tells us that the consequence of this can be wholly contrary to the wishes of the voters themselves, taken individually. This is most clear, for example, where the majority opinion of the population is in favour of the market economy, but where a majority also has a more specific interest in seeing it limited or replaced in a particular case. 'In such conditions', he writes,

> a political party hoping to achieve and maintain power will have little choice but to use its powers to buy the support of particular groups. They will do so not because the majority is interventionist, but because the ruling party would not retain a majority if it did not buy the support of particular groups by the promise of special benefits.[26]

This, of course, would not be a particularly acute problem if the government were limited by laws that determined how resources would be put at its disposal but over which it had no control. But, 'it assumes alarming proportions', Hayek claims, 'when government and rule-making come to be confused and the persons who administer the resources of government also determine how much of the *total* resources it ought to control'.[27] This process is exemplified by Hayek with reference to the example of social justice where 'traditional barriers to arbitrary use of power were at first penetrated from entirely benevolent motives'.[28] Government acting directly to assist the less well-off thus began to be action that violated one of the cornerstones of the rule of law: equal treatment under the law. As we saw in his critique of social justice, 'in order to put into a more equal material position people who are inevitably very different in many of the conditions on which their worldly success depends it is necessary to treat them unequally'.[29] More significantly, opening the door up to government activity in this way meant that the government itself became vulnerable to intense political pressure.[30]

Hayek's critique would seem to imply that he is an opponent of democracy and deeply sceptical of the motives of politicians. Yet, despite his criticisms, Hayek is no anti-democrat. In *The Constitution of Liberty* he explicitly rejects this label and makes three arguments in favour of democracy centred on its procedural advantage in effecting political change without violence, its safeguarding of individual liberty and its educative function.[31] Furthermore, and just as he is not willing to reject democracy as 'an ideal worth fighting for to the utmost, because it is our only protection (even if in its present from not a certain one) against tyranny', Hayek also contends that parties and politicians should not be blamed for the problems of modern liberal democracy. A political leader may in fact be motivated by the highest of motives. However, in order to achieve his aims he needs power, and to enjoy this in a democracy,

> he needs the support of a majority which he can get only by enlisting people who are little interested in the objectives which guide him. To build up support for his programme he will therefore have to offer effective enticements to a sufficient number of special interests to bring together a majority for the support of his programme as a whole.[32]

'We have no right', Hayek concludes, 'to blame the politicians for doing what they must do in the position in which we have placed them' because it is us who 'have created the conditions in which it is known that the majority has power to give any particular section of the population whatever it demands'.[33] The root of the problem, therefore, is not a moral one – although its consequences may nevertheless be morally unappealing – but rather institutional and structural. The problem that Hayek identifies with modern democratic government is not to be found in the motivations of the elected official, or for that matter, of the self-interested voter or interest group. It is to be found in the unconstrained and unlimited nature of the democratic power that connects the governors and the governed.[34]

Significantly, the problem that Hayek identifies leads him to make what is perhaps a surprising claim about the state. Paradoxically, the supposedly omnipotent democratic state 'becomes as a result of unlimited powers *exceedingly weak*, the playball of all these separate interests it has to satisfy to secure majority support'.[35] The dangers attendant to a political structure that remained unprotected from the partiality of the omnipotent monarch, we discover, have not been banished but merely transferred into the impersonal structural organization of the liberal democratic state, where decisions about what is to count as law and what the government should do are made by either the same body, or by two different bodies comprised in the same way. We can also give an epistemological explanation of the reason why special interest politics and unlimited government is problematic for Hayek. Such a democracy is not only weak in the sense he describes, but also unavoidably oversteps the cultivating role Hayek says is appropriate for it, to the detriment of its epistemological and coordinative function. By granting resources to particular interests, the government not only disregards that knowledge held by others outside of the group about the circumstances that would otherwise be relevant to a wider, properly social, determination of where resources should go. In doing so, it ends up misdirecting those resources. Thus Hayek concludes that '[w]e can prevent government from serving special interests only by depriving it of the power to use coercion in doing so', or, in other words, 'we can limit the powers of organized interests only by limiting the powers of government' in which the legislature is confined to laying down general rules and the government can only use coercion to enforce but not change them.[36] It is to this project of rescuing liberal democratic government from itself, by setting out in explicit terms how the tasks of stating what the law is and of day-to-day governance can be separated, that Hayek turns his attention in his theory of the ideal, or model, constitution.

A Model Constitution

The Basic Clause of the constitution

'Government', wrote Hayek towards the end of his career, and drawing together many of the principal themes of his intellectual journey, 'is of necessity the product of intellectual design'.[37] How, then, do his views about status of knowledge in a complex society colour his approach to the issue of the model constitution?[38] Central here is his idea of the state's appropriate role being that of cultivator rather than director of the circumstances conducive to spontaneous socio-economic order. Not only is his model constitution the summation of his ideas about how there can be a healthy relationship between the individual and the organization that is the state, in which democracy 'operates as a safeguard of personal freedom because it accepts the limitations of a higher nomos', and where the state cultivates the environment for, but does not determine the particular outcomes of, the socio-economic process.[39] Equally significantly, the model constitution is also the conclusion of Hayek's thought on the role of reason with respect to social organization.

Clearly, and given his ideas about the defects of modern democratic government, Hayek is not prepared to defend the democratic *status quo* as a part of this project. Nevertheless, and beyond claiming that it is an ideal worth fighting for, Hayek is 'profoundly disturbed by the rapid decline of faith' in democracy and is 'anxious to rescue the true ideal from the miscredit into which it is falling'.[40] In *The Constitution of Liberty*, Hayek provides an idea of democratic government's ideal form when he notes the importance of separating the functions of the direction of the day-to-day affairs of the government from that of stating what the law is.[41] It is in *The Political Order of a Free People*, however, that he sets out in detail his theory of a model liberal constitution. In its broadest features this constitution is made up of a Basic Clause, a bicameral system of government consisting of a lower house, or Governmental Assembly, an upper house, or Legislative Assembly, and of a Constitutional Court. In keeping with the importance of the distinction between law and legislation, as well as to rectify what he understands to be the failure of contemporary democracy to effectively separate powers, the aim of this constitution is to 'secure a real separation of powers between two distinct representative bodies whereby law-making in the narrow sense as well as government proper would be conducted democratically, *but by different and mutually independent agencies*'.[42]

At the most general level, the Basic Clause of the constitution 'defines what can be substantive law in order to allocate and limit powers among the parts of the organization it sets up'. Importantly, however, it 'leaves the *content* of this law to be developed by the legislature and judiciary' and therefore represents no more than

> a protective superstructure designed to regulate the continuous process of developing an existing body of law and to prevent any confusion of the powers of government in enforcing rules on which the spontaneous order of society rests, and those of using the material means entrusted to its administration for the rendering of services to the individuals and groups.[43]

In brief, then, the Basic Clause of the constitution represents Hayek's idea of 'dividing the supreme power between two distinct democratically elect assemblies, i.e. by applying the principle of the separation of powers on the highest level'.[44]

To achieve this Hayek divides the Basic Clause into two parts. Firstly, it states that citizens could be restrained from doing as they wished, and ordered to do particular things, only in accordance with the rules of just conduct. Secondly it stipulates that the only body allowed to deliberately alter those rules is the Legislative Assembly. As an additional safeguard and to sever the connection between the source of legislation and its legitimacy, the Basic Clause would also contain an explicit definition of *nomos* to enable the Constitutional Court to decide whether a law passed by the Legislative Assembly conformed to its basic properties. The content of this definition essentially tracks the six criteria of sound law which we saw Hayek sets out in his legal theory.[45] Importantly, the Basic Clause would not say what functions were properly governmental ones but, rather, would merely define the limits of its coercive functions. The definition of the proper sphere of governmental activity, therefore, is not achieved directly but rather through the imposition of constitutional side-constraints on the way in which government may carry out its day-to-day duties.[46] Hayek's hope, moreover, is that the Basic Clause would achieve more than a Bill of Rights, which in his view, can only ever be unhelpfully selective with respect to the kinds of rights that are protected.[47] Rather than draw up a list of such rights considered worthy of special protection, and thus run the risk of signalling that those not included may be violated, for Hayek it is preferable to have no list at all and instead define what can count as a law.

The Governmental Assembly

Mindful of the fact that central to this constitutional scheme is the restoration of the distinction between the direction of governmental activity and the passing of laws that (indirectly) define the scope of that activity, Hayek suggests dividing government into two separate, independent assemblies: a lower house – or Governmental Assembly – which looks after the interests of the citizens who elect it and is responsible for the day-to-day affairs of government, and an upper house, or Legislative Assembly that passes laws in addition to and where necessary, corrective of, those that emerge in the common law. The function of these two democratically elected assemblies is to separate the concrete *will* and *interest* of the citizens in particular results from general *opinion* about what kinds of governmental action are right or wrong. This is necessary, according to Hayek, to avoid the possibility evidenced in his critique of majoritarian democracy that the interest of the majority achieves the status of law simply because it is its will that it be so. For Hayek, laws are to codify, pre-existing and customary rules of just conduct, rather than to push through the interests of particular groups, and it is the job of the two distinct chambers to see that this remains so.

The Governmental Assembly is modelled on contemporary parliaments and would be the centre of government and party politics as we know it. Indeed, precisely because it is charged with achieving a specific particular purpose, namely the day-to-day direction of government, the Governmental Assembly would be organized along party political lines.[48] The effectiveness of the Governmental Assembly, that is, is predicated upon there existing within it 'a majority of members agreed on a programme of action' because 'the effective direction of the whole apparatus of government, or the control of the use of all the personal and material resources placed under its supervision, demands the continuous support of the executive authority by an organized majority committed to a coherent plan of action'.[49] Nevertheless, the Governmental Assembly would be bound by the rules of just conduct as laid down by the Legislative Assembly and could not compel citizens via legislation in ways which were inconsistent with those rules.[50] Within these limits, however, the governing party of the Legislative Assembly would be 'complete master in organizing the apparatus of government and deciding about the use of material and personal resources entrusted to the government', just as they are in contemporary liberal democratic states.[51]

These similarities notwithstanding, Hayek's account of the Governmental Assembly is in an important respect highly idiosyncratic. Most strikingly, he suggests that suffrage for this chamber should be non-universal, with employees of the state, civil servants, pensioners and the unemployed, *not* being permitted to vote for its representatives.[52] To contemporary sensibilities, such a recommendation sounds, at the very least, odd, if not disturbing. The reason for this recommendation for what is in effect a violation of one of the basic rights of citizenship, relates back to Hayek's desire to separate decision-making based on *interest* from that based on *opinion*. The problem here is that allowing recipients of government funds an effective say in the running and composition of the government itself would be to risk its capture by organized and ever-expanding interests. It is for this reason that Hayek contends that giving civil servants, old age pensioners and the unemployed the right to 'vote on how they should be paid out of the pocket of the rest is hardly a reasonable arrangement'.[53] Despite the logic of his argument, this position is in an important respect necessitated by Hayek's defence of direct state provision of an economic minimum and relates back to the weakness of his engagement with social justice. Having such a statutory minimum can only but create an electoral constituency whose primary political interest would be in seeing that it remains, or increases. Of course, even if he ruled such a minimum out, he would still be in a similar position with regard to state employees, a problem which, it seems reasonable to claim, renders his proposal politically unfeasible.

The Legislative Assembly and the Constitutional Court

In contrast to the Governmental Assembly, the upper house or Legislative Assembly is charged not with directing government but with revising 'the body of private (including commercial and criminal) law'.[54] It is in this sense, then, that along with common law judges, and the judges of the Constitutional Court, the Legislative Assembly represents the institutional embodiment of the cultivating role of the state. Importantly, one of the reasons Hayek thinks the British system ultimately failed to secure the separation of the power to legislate from that of the direction of government that this cultivating role requires was because the upper House of Lords – the equivalent of the Legislative Assembly in Hayek's scheme – represented but a small privileged class.[55]

For this reason Hayek proposes an elected Upper House but, in order
to obtain a similar independence from political pressure that the historical House of Lords enjoyed by being unelected, and to ensure that
the Legislative Assembly is able to provide an effective check upon the
decisions of the Governmental Assembly, he claims that the membership of each respective body not be composed in the same way.[56] The
reason for this is that if the two assemblies were merely charged with
different tasks, but composed of approximately the same proportions
of representatives from the same groups or parties, there would be a
danger that the Legislative Assembly would merely provide those laws
which the Governmental Assembly wanted. The consequence of this,
of course would be to effectively collapse the bicameral system into a
unitary one, thus defeating the fundamental aim of a separation of
powers between legitimate law-making and governance that is central
to Hayek's constitutional theory.[57]

Hayek makes a number of suggestions to secure a differenti-
ated composition of the members of the two chambers. Firstly,
elections to the Legislative Assembly would be held once a year
to select one-fifteenth of the Assembly for a fifteen-year term. The
elected members should be respected because of their performance in professional and public life. They should, Hayek somewhat oddly asserts, be honest and their salary should 'be fixed by
the Constitution at a certain percentage of the average of say, the
twenty most highly paid posts in the gift of government' in order to
guarantee representatives a carefree future after tenure and thus
make them resistant to bribery.[58] As an extra safeguard, he suggests
that ex-members of the Governmental Assembly should not be permitted to enter the Legislative Assembly. Significantly, however,
and similarly to his suggestions for the Governmental Assembly,
Hayek suggests that the franchise for the Legislative Assembly be
restricted in two senses. Firstly, that electors vote for members of
the Legislative Assembly only once in their lives and that this be
in the year when they become 45 years old. Despite the obvious
objection that this would be discriminatory, Hayek claims that even
though the under 45s would not be represented, the average age
of the members – 52-and-a-half – would actually be lower than that
of most parliaments. Indeed, he makes this suggestion precisely
in order to avoid having too many 'old persons' in the chamber.[59]
Regardless, however, of this suggestion's other possible merits,

there is no guarantee in any case that the 52-and-a-half year thresh-
old would not be surpassed without enacting Hayek's scheme. In a
similar vein, Hayek contends that the two assemblies should be governed by different norms.[60] Given that the task of the Governmental
Assembly is to attend to the concrete wishes of the people, it is
only right and proper that it is governed by *interest*. However, the
Legislative Assembly, which is to act as a check upon the action of
the Governmental Assembly would be governed by another norm
in the interests of the separation of powers. For the Legislative
Assembly, then, Hayek contends that it needs to be governed by
general majority *opinion* about what is right and wrong and not by
the interests of more narrowly defined groups.[61]

Beyond any misgivings we may have about the age restrictions,
another objection to the Legislative Assembly is that if it were
charged with merely deciding the law, it would have very little to do.
Yet, although concerned in the main with corrections of private law
(commercial and criminal) Hayek claims that all enforceable rules of
conduct would have to have the sanction of the Legislative Assembly.
These will include

> not only the principles of *taxation* but also all those regulations of
> *safety and health*, including regulations of production or construc-
> tion, that have to be enforced in the general interest and should be
> stated in the form of general rules. These comprise not only what
> used to be called safety legislation but also all the difficult problems
> of *creating an adequate framework for a functioning competitive market* and
> *the law of corporations*.[62]

These, he notes, are not matters of administration but of legislation
proper. That is, they are regulation (of the private acts of individuals on the market). Hayek also claims that it is preferential that this
function be the preserve of the Legislative Assembly rather than of
the governmental bureaucracy so as to avoid that latter acquiring too
much power for itself.

Finally, Hayek sets out the responsibilities of the Constitutional Court
whose primary task is to determine which of the Legislative Assembly
and Governmental Assembly is authorized to pass a particular resolution, as well as whether anybody at all is authorized to pass it.[63] In
effect, then, the Constitutional Court would be charged with resolving

practical difficulties in maintaining the integrity of the distinction at the heart of Hayek's constitutional enterprise

> between the enforceable rules of just conduct to be developed by the Legislative Assembly and binding government and citizens alike, and all those rules of the organization and conduct of government proper which, within the limits of the law, it would be the task of the Governmental Assembly to determine.[64]

Evaluation of Hayek's constitutional proposals

What, then, are we to make of Hayek's constitutional proposals? Firstly, they may not secure the kind of classical liberal polity Hayek is seeking. Indeed, he contends that they are neutral and 'consistent with a number of alternative societies'.[65] Similarly, it has been contended that Hayek's proposals offer no sure protection against illiberal legislation.[66] The issue here lies principally with the function of the Legislative Assembly. To be sure, it would rule out the most robust forms of central planning, and 'pork-barrel socialism' that are reliant on the issuing of direct commands, for these would be formally inadmissible by the Basic Clause.[67] Yet, as several commentators contend, Hayek's proposals are nonetheless indeterminate because it would still be possible to frame laws to permit forms of socialism or other 'injunctions totally incompatible with individual liberty', so long as these took the general form which Hayek argues the rules of just conduct ought to take in order to be considered legitimate.[68]

Yet, it seems that these misgivings are exaggerated for at least two reasons. First, it is doubtful that the Legislative Assembly would be more activist than Hayek himself envisions. The vast majority of work pertinent to the definition of individual domains would be carried out via the common law legal system and not the Legislative Assembly. The common law, of course, is itself based on the articulation of *non*-command-like rules of just conduct, so there is reason to believe that the kinds of rules in operation would be just the kind Hayek envisions. Moreover, and as we have seen, it is only in the event of what Hayek calls evolutionary dead ends. Or in circumstances in which the common law does not evolve quickly enough, that the Legislative Assembly would step in. Yet even here it would be limited with respect to the kind of law that it could pass. Crucial here is Hayek's claim that it is *not* just in its formulation that the law would have to avoid mention of particular individuals, interests or groups. Regardless of that form, it would also have to do so insofar as its *effects* were concerned. Thus, a law that for example stipulated that 'all persons capable of becoming pregnant are not allowed to own property' would be just as unacceptable to Hayek's system as would the laws of couverture.

Nevertheless, and regardless of the persuasiveness of these counter-objections, it seems reasonable to conclude that the age-restriction for the Legislative Assembly and the lack of universal suffrage for the Governmental Assembly would, in the modern era, prove to be insurmountable obstacles to the adoption of Hayek's scheme, both in moral terms and, indeed, in the democratic sense that voters would be highly unlikely to give up the franchise in the form they presently enjoy. Indeed, when compared to his theory of the rule of law, the administrative laws of organization relating to the scope of the franchise which Hayek suggests for the two democratic chambers are oddly exemplary of the very kinds of specific, group-naming practices that he claims persuasively elsewhere are to be avoided.

The unfeasibility of Hayek's constitutional proposals, moreover, points us to perhaps a more serious problem relating to the theme of the proper role of the state that emerges from his unique epistemological analysis of complex societies. Despite the original and fruitful paradigm he provides for establishing and discussing in new ways many of the most important problems in modern political theory, Hayek's failure to deliver a feasible theory of the constitutional liberal democratic state means that his project does not ultimately pass the test it sets itself. This, moreover, is not simply a problem that affects but one aspect of his contribution. Precisely because his research programme points so tellingly to the issue of the appropriate use of reason in determining the role of the state under complex social conditions, Hayek's constitutional theory is the contribution upon which, in an important sense, the rest of his normative project hangs. Its failure, if indeed it does fail, means that the powers of human reason that he undoubtedly believes in will have to be deployed anew if the test of determining, via the use of reason, what the state should and should not do is to be passed. To be sure, there is a big difference between the merits of a specific constitutional theory and the philosophical perspective from which it emerges. With this in mind, it remains now to consider the reception and influence of Hayek's ideas and the relevance, if any, his research programme may have today.

Notes

[1] Hayek, *The Constitution of Liberty*, chapter 7; *The Political Order of a Free People*, London, Routledge, 1979, chapters 12, 13 and 16.

[2] Hayek, 'The Constitution of a Liberal State', in Hayek, F.A. (ed.), *New Studies in Philosophy, Politics, Economics and the History of Ideas*, London, Routledge and Kegan Paul, (1967c) 1978, p. 98, 'Whither Democracy?', in Hayek, F. A. (ed), *New Studies in Philosophy, Politics, Economics and the History of Ideas*, London, Routledge and Kegan Paul, (1976d) 1978, pp. 153–154. The word 'arbitrary', of course, signifies a judgment made at the discretion of the *arbiter*, rather than with reference to general principles.

[3] Hayek, 'Whither Democracy?', p. 155; See also Hayek, 'The Constitution of a Liberal State', p. 99.

[4] Ibid., pp. 152–153.

[5] Ibid., pp. 153.

[6] de Tocqueville, A., *Democracy in America*, London, Penguin Classics, (1835/1840) 2003.

[7] Mill, J. S., *On Liberty*, pp. 6–8; *Considerations on Representative Government*, London, Everyman, (1861) 1993, pp. 269–270.

[8] Hayek, *The Political Order of a Free People*, pp. 2–3. See also Hayek, The *Constitution of Liberty*, p. 107.

[9] Ibid., p. 6, emphasis added.

[10] Ibid., pp. 105–106; 'Economic Freedom and Representative Government', p. 115; 'Whither Democracy?', pp. 154–155.

[11] Ibid., p. 1, emphasis added.

[12] Mill, *On Liberty*, p. 8; Hayek, 'Economic Freedom and Representative Government', p. 109, 110; *The Constitution of Liberty*, p. 107.

[13] Hayek, *The Constitution of Liberty*, pp. 106, 155–156. See also, Hayek, *The Political Order of a Free People*, p. 31.

[14] Hayek, 'The Constitution of a Liberal State', p. 101.

[15] Ibid., p. 104. See also, Hayek, *The Road to Serfdom*, p. 71.

[16] Ibid., pp. 98, 101; See also Hayek, 'Economic Freedom and Representative Government', p. 114.

[17] Ibid., p. 99. See also Hayek, 'Economic Freedom and Representative Government', p. 115; *The Constitution of Liberty*, p. 207; 'Whither Democracy?', p. 154.

[18] Hayek, *The Political Order of a Free People*, p. 8.

[19] Ibid., p. 4, emphasis added. See also, p. 8; Hayek, *The Constitution of Liberty*, p. 207; 'The Constitution of a Liberal State', p. 98.

[20] Ibid., original emphasis. See also Hayek, 'Economic Freedom and Representative Government', p. 112; 'Whither Democracy?', p. 155.

[21] Hayek, *The Road to Serfdom*, p. 71, emphasis added.

[22] Hayek, *The Political Order of a Free People*, p. 13. See also Hayek, 'The Constitution of a Liberal State', p. 100; 'Economic Freedom and Representative Government', p. 114; 'Whither Democracy?', p. 156.

[23] Ibid., p. 13.

[24] Ibid., p. 16.

[25] Ibid., p. 99. See also Hayek, 'The Constitution of a Liberal State', p. 100; Hayek, F. A., 'Will the Democratic Ideal Prevail?', in Hayek, F. A. (ed.), *Economic Freedom*, Cambridge, Blackwell, (1978) 1991, p. 403.

[26] Hayek, 'Economic Freedom and Representaive Government', pp. 107–108.

[27] Hayek, *The Political Order of a Free People*, p. 16, emphasis added.

[28] Ibid., p.103.

[29] Ibid.

[30] Hayek, 'The Constitution of a Liberal State', p. 100.

[31] Hayek, *The Constitution of Liberty*, pp. 107–109, 115–117.

[32] Hayek, *The Political Order of a Free People*, p. 15. See also Hayek, 'Economic Freedom and Representative Government', pp. 107–108.

[33] Ibid. See also Hayek, 'Will the Democratic Ideal Prevail?', p. 404.

[34] Ibid. See also Hayek, 'Economic Freedom and Representative Government', pp. 107–108.

[35] Ibid., emphasis added, 129; See also Hayek, 'Whither Democracy?', pp. 156–157;'Will the Democratic Ideal Prevail?', p. 400.

[36] Ibid., p.16.

[37] Ibid., p. 152.

[38] Ibid., p. 2.

[39] Ibid.

[40] Ibid., p. 5; See also Hayek, 'Will the Democratic Ideal Prevail?', p. 399; 'Wither Democracy?', p. 152.

[41] Hayek, *The Constitution of Liberty*, p. 207. See also Hayek, *The Political Ideal of the Rule of Law*, pp. 37–41; 'The Constitution of a Liberal State', p. 99; 'Will the Democratic Ideal Prevail?' p. 402.

[42] Hayek, *The Political Order of a Free People*, p. 107, emphasis added.

[43] Ibid., p. 122.

[44] Hayek, 'Will the Democratic Ideal Prevail?', p. 405.

[45] Hayek, *The Political Order of a Free People*, p. 109, emphasis added.

[46] Ibid., p. 110.

[47] Ibid., pp. 110–111. See also Hayek, *The Road to Serfdom*, pp. 84–85 where Hayek's view is less sceptical of the efficaciousness of a Bill of Rights in securing the Rule of Law.

[48] Hayek, 'The Constitution of a Liberal State', p. 102.

[49] Hayek, *The Political Order of a Free People*, p. 23.

[50] Ibid., p. 119.

[51] Ibid.

[52] Ibid., p. 120. See also Hayek, The *Constitution of Liberty*, p. 105.

[53] Ibid.

[54] Ibid., p.114.

[55] Ibid., p.106. See also Hayek, 'Whither Democracy?', p. 155.

[56] Hayek, 'The Constitution of a Liberal State', p. 102, 'Economic Freedom and Representative Government', pp. 115–116; 'Whither Democracy?', p. 159.

[57] Hayek, *The Political Order of a Free People*, p. 112; 'Economic Freedom and Representative Government', p. 116.

58 Ibid., p. 114. See also Hayek, 'The Constitution of a Liberal State', pp. 102–103, 'Economic Freedom and Representative Government', pp. 116–117, 'Whither Democracy?', pp. 160–161.

59 Ibid., p. 113.

60 Hayek, 'Economic Freedom and Representative Government', p. 117.

61 Hayek, *The Political Order of a Free People*, p. 112; *The Constitution of Liberty*, pp. 109–110; 'The Constitution of a Liberal State', p. 102, 'Economic Freedom and Representative Government', p. 117.

62 Hayek, *The Political Order of a Free People*, p. 115, emphasis added.

63 Ibid., p.121; 'Economic Freedom and Representative Government', p. 118; 'Whither Democracy?', p. 160.

64 Ibid., p.120.

65 Gamble, A., *Hayek: The Iron Cage of Liberty*, Boulder, Westview Press, 1996, p. 149.

66 Bellamy, *Liberalism and Pluralism: Towards a Politics of Compromise*, London, Routledge, 1999, pp. 32–33.

67 Gamble, *Hayek: The Iron Cage of Liberty*, p. 149.

68 Ibid.

6

Reception, Influence and Contemporary Relevance

Intellectual and Political Influence

Keynes, the socialist calculation debate and equilibrium

There are two key aspects to any assessment of the reception and influence of Hayek's ideas. First it is necessary to examine the impact of his contributions to the specific academic debates in which he participated. These, we have seen in the preceding chapters, were made across a wide variety of fields of enquiry during his long career. Beyond this more obvious academic assessment of his influence, however, it is also important for at least two reasons to assess Hayek's impact upon the world of politics and policy. This is so in the first instance because, given that he was both an economist and a political theorist, much of what he had to say had a direct bearing upon fundamental questions of social organization. In addition and beyond the fact that he was intellectually concerned with worldly affairs, assessing Hayek from this more historical standpoint is also important because, from quite early on in his career, he was not only an academic and intellectual but also an intellectual *activist* who was concerned with the worldly influence of ideas, including his own.

Hayek's influence upon the development of economics was recognized by the award of the Nobel Prize in Economics in 1974, earned jointly with Swedish economist Gunnar Myrdal, 'for their pioneering work in the theory of money and economic fluctuations and for their penetrating analysis of the interdependence of economic, social and institutional phenomena'.[1] Despite the obvious honour, Hayek was somewhat surprised to receive the Nobel Prize.[2] Economics, after all, had not been his central interest for some 30 years. Yet, there is no doubting that, after arriving at the LSE in 1931, Hayek was, along with his Cambridge friend and rival Keynes, for a few years very influential in economics, principally because of this work on the trade cycle and capital theory. Ultimately, however, he was to lose out to Keynes to whose side most of the faculty and research students even at the LSE had switched by the end of the 1930s.[3] Indeed, whilst the macroeconomic approach of Keynesianism assumed the status of orthodoxy throughout the liberal democratic world in the post-war era, Hayek's Austrian contributions, that emphasized instead the individual microfoundations of economic behaviour, became largely forgotten.

The reasons for this decline are related to two important debates in which Hayek participated and about which the general consensus was that he had came off worst. The first of these was his debate with Keynes in the 1930s over the question of the business cycle, the second with Oscar Lange, in the late 1930s and the 1940s, over the economics of socialism. Central to Hayek's rejection of Keynes' discourse on the business cycle in *A Treatise on Money* was the latter's contention that the market could not maintain equality between the rate of saving and investment and, as such, was incapable of adjusting to structural shifts in demand. For this reason, Keynes maintained, the state had to play an active role in manipulating the money supply, and with it aggregate demand, so that the cycle of boom and bust could be avoided.[4] This, of course, was the opposite of Hayek's view, which claimed that it was government interference which caused the cycle to occur because it distorted the structure of production in an unsustainable manner.[5] There then ensued a sometimes heated exchange of views, both in journals such as *Economica*, and in written correspondence between Hayek and Keynes.[6] Significantly, Keynes' final letter to Hayek explained that he was revising his central position as set out in the *Treatise*. Some years later Keynes published *The General Theory of Employment, Money and Interest*, perhaps the most important treatise on economics since Smith's *The Wealth of Nations*.[7]

One of the reasons why Hayek was considered to have lost the debate about the business cycle with Keynes was because he never responded to the *General Theory*. His own reason for this was twofold. Firstly, given that in his correspondence Keynes appeared to be in the process of changing his mind with respect to the *Treatise*, Hayek decided not to respond to the *General Theory* in any detailed manner lest this happen again.[8] Yet, perhaps more tellingly, Hayek also noted that another, more persuasive, reason was because of his fundamental disagreement with

Keynes' basic premises. As an Austrian theorist who had always empha-sized the microfoundations of economic behaviour, Hayek would have had little sympathy with Keynes macroeconomic approach, as he regarded as misconceived the attempt to study as complex a structure as the economy through macro level aggregates. As Gamble has noted '[t]his methodological objection made [Hayek] unsympathetic to the problems which Keynes was trying to solve, and disinclined to become involved in detailed technical debate, given that he did not accept the premises from which Keynes was starting'.[9] The problem for Hayek, however, was that the exact nature of his disagreement was not alto-gether clear to him at the time.[10] In any case, and regardless of exactly why he did not respond to it, the undoubted consequence of Hayek's not doing so was that it appeared that he had ceded the ground to Keynesianism.[11]

The second important debate in economics to which Hayek con-tributed was the socialist calculation debate about the possibility of rational economic calculation in the absence of a price system. As we saw in Chapter 3 this debate was actually initiated by Mises and con-tinued by Lange. Moreover, we saw that it was in the course of his engagement with Lange that Hayek is credited with introducing the notion of time to the theoretical construction of equilibrium, and thus for drawing attention to economic theory's need to give an account of how information relevant to rational economic calculation is actu-ally transferred across the economy, in this case in the form of prices. Yet, despite the cogency of his arguments, their impact was limited. Again, similar, to his disagreement with Keynes on the trade cycle, the Austrian microeconomic perspective from which Hayek was arguing was so fundamentally at odds with the neoclassical one of his interlocu-tors that much of what he had to say was simply dismissed.[12] In both cases, it may well be that the explanation for Hayek's gradual abandon-ment of formal economics and increasing forays into social and politi-cal theory can be traced to this change in his intellectual fortunes, as well as the consequent desire to state in more general terms the Knowledge Problem that informed his opposition to the arguments of Keynes and Lange.[13]

Hayek was to dedicate virtually the rest of his career to this broader project and it is for the fruits of his investigations that he is best known today. Thus, despite the events of his own career, Hayek's view of the market as a spontaneous information-processing and self-correcting system has turned out to be one of the more important political insights of the twentieth century. Equally important from an historical perspective, Hayek's contribution was not only theoretically significant but has since come to play an important role in our understanding of historical events, most notably the collapse of the communist regimes of central and eastern Europe in the late 1980s and early 1990s. Of course, whilst it would be outlandish to claim some direct causal relationship between Hayek's ideas on equilibrium, the epistemological function of the market and the fall of the Berlin Wall, his thought can be seen with good reason to provide at least one very powerful explanation of the seismic change that the events of 1989 represented.

The Road to Serfdom and *The Constitution of Liberty*

Hayek's intellectual activism can be clearly seen in the publication of *The Road to Serfdom* in 1944, and his warning about the dangers to liberal democracy in attempting to run a centrally planned economy. No less an authority than Keynes – the man with whom we have seen Hayek vied in the 1930s and early 1940s as the most influential economist in the world – stated in a letter to Hayek that *The Road to Serfdom* was

> a grand book. We all have the greatest reason to be grateful to you for saying so well what needs so much to be said. You will not expect me to accept quite all the economic dicta in it. But morally and philosophically I find myself in agreement with virtually the whole of it; and not only in agreement with it, but in deeply moved agreement.[14]

Similarly, the novelist and journalist George Orwell responded to the book in a positive fashion by saying in a 1944 review that 'in the negative part of Professor Hayek's thesis there is a great deal of truth. It cannot be said too often – at any rate, it is not being said nearly often enough – that collectivism is not inherently democratic, but, on the contrary, gives to a tyrannical minority such powers as the Spanish Inquisitors never dreamt of'.[15]

Perhaps unexpectedly *The Road to Serfdom* was an astonishing popular success, launching Hayek on a trajectory of notoriety, particularly in the United States.[16] It was also not without its detractors. Indeed, Orwell also said in the same review that 'a return to "free" competition means for the great mass of people a tyranny probably worse, because more irresponsible than that of the state' and that the capitalism that Hayek defended 'leads to dole queues, the scramble for markets and war'.[17] Moreover, in academic circles many of Hayek's peers viewed it as a polemical text, despite it being conceived as the fourth and final part of larger project about the theoretical and practical influence of 'scientism'. Most notably Hayek's colleague at the LSE, and political scientist, Herman Finer wrote a particularly trenchant critique of the book entitled *The Road to Reaction* in which, among other things, he described Hayek as having 'a thoroughly Hitlerian contempt for democratic man', that moved Hayek to write that Finer's book was 'a specimen of abuse and invective which is probably unique in contemporary academic discussion'.[18] Similarly, in the *American Political Science Review* Charles Merriam denounced *The Road to Serfdom* as a 'confused', 'cynical', and 'over-rated work of little permanent value' and 'one of the strange survivals of obscurantism in modern times'. In the *New Republic* Alvin H. Hansen, the leading American exponent of Keynesian economics, published a four-page critique which concluded: 'Hayek's book will not be long lived. There is no substance in it to make it live', and conceded only that it would 'momentarily' arouse discussion and prompt some useful 'self-examination'. Meanwhile, the editorial columns of the *New Republic* asserted that the heavy sales of *The Road to Serfdom* were coming from orders placed by 'business interests' who were using Hayek's 'doctrine' to defend practices of which the professor himself disapproved. Hayek's worldly success, it sniffed, 'amounts to little more than an indignity'. A less acerbic rebuttal came from Barbara Wootton much of whose *Freedom under Planning* was directed against Hayek's argument.[19]

The reception of the book affected Hayek both personally and professionally. He said later that he 'long resented being more widely known by what I regarded as a pamphlet for the time than by my strictly scientific work' and it was this that prompted him to restart work on the project that became *The Sensory Order*, in the desire to rehabilitate what he saw as damage to his intellectual reputation.[20] Moreover, another substantive issue that Keynes had with *The Road to Serfdom* and which he expressed to Hayek in the same letter where he had praised the book, also helped to set Hayek onto a different intellectual course. Keynes' concern was that *The Road to Serfdom* was comprised largely of critique which, despite emphasizing the importance of distinguishing between the agenda and non-agenda of government, actually provided little practical guidance as to how this ought to be done.[21] In response to this challenge Hayek began work on his first substantial positive defence of the classical liberal ideal of individual liberty. The result of that effort was *The Constitution of Liberty*. Hayek had very high expectations for this book upon its publication in 1960 but these were to be disappointed. In a review in the *New York Times Book Review* Sydney Hook stated that 'as a cautionary voice Mr. Hayek is always worth listening to. He is an intellectual tonic. But in our present time of troubles, his economic philosophy points the road to disaster' and Anthony Quinton, a British philosopher, dismissed it as a 'magnificent dinosaur'.[22] Reviews by Hayek's former colleague Lionel Robbins, as well as by Jacob Viner, Frank Knight and Ronald Hamowy were also broadly critical. In the case of Robbins, Knight and Viner this was because of Hayek's overwhelming emphasis upon freedom at the expense of other values, whilst Hamowy contended that he did not go far enough in endorsing that liberty.[23] Nevertheless, over the longer term *The Constitution of Liberty* and his later trilogy *Law, Legislation and Liberty* were to seal Hayek's place, along with Robert Nozick, as one of the two most important defenders of the classical liberal/libertarian position in the twentieth century. In a letter to the *Times Literary Supplement*, Popper remonstrated against this publication for not reviewing the trilogy first volume, *Rules and Order*, stating that 'Hayek's book is a new opening of the most fundamental debate in the field of political philosophy'.[24]

Intellectual activism and politics

Despite the often negative reaction to Hayek's thought and the increasing academic isolation in which he found himself subsequent to the publication of *The Road to Serfdom*, the post-war period also saw Hayek's name feature more frequently in political discussion. In an infamous episode of the 1945 general election campaign Winston Churchill claimed, apparently after having read Hayek's book, that in order to achieve their aims, the Labour Party would ultimately have to rely upon a Gestapo because '[n]o socialist system can be established without a political police'. Needless to say, coming so soon after the conclusion of the struggle against Nazi Germany, the comment backfired. Outraged, his opponent and former colleague in the war-time coalition government, Clement Attlee, retorted that Churchill was enunciating 'the second-hand version of the academic views of

an Austrian professor, Friedrich August von Hayek', apparently oblivi-
ous to the fact that all particles denoting nobility such as 'von' were
outlawed in Austria, along with the nobility and its legal privileges, in
1919.[25]

Any influence that Hayek exerted in the postwar era was perhaps most significant with Margaret Thatcher, both as leader of the
Opposition and as Prime Minister, and whose 11 years of power has
in turn exerted a profound influence upon the direction of British
politics ever since. There was perhaps no better indication of Hayek's
influence than when Thatcher attended a Conservative Party strategy
meeting in which a paper was presented that argued for the Tories
to adopt a 'middle way' between left and right. The new Leader of
the Opposition is said to have reached into her bag and brandished
a copy of *The Constitution of Liberty*. 'This', she said sternly, 'is what we
believe' and banged the book onto the table.[26] Of course, to many
Hayek's influence was nothing but pernicious, so much so that in 1978
Thatcher was attacked by the then Leader of the House of Commons
and future Leader of the Labour Party, Michael Foot, as being in the
thrall of Hayek, 'the mad professor'.[27]

Whilst never enjoying any formal position even at an advisory level
in Thatcher's government, Hayek's thought undoubtedly also influenced her on a policy level. Soon after Thatcher came to power in
1979 Hayek argued in an Institute of Economic Affairs pamphlet, *1980s
Unemployment and the Unions*, that the extensive power then enjoyed
by the trade unions was one of the primary causes of unemployment
because of its discoordinating effects upon the labour market. His
conclusion was that one way of addressing this would be to make
membership of unions voluntary and remove their legal privileges.[28]
Legislation subsequently introduced by Thatcher limited the power
of the trade unions by curbing the rights of picketers and holding
national union organizations financially responsible for actions taken
at the local level. Moreover, Thatcher rejected the Keynesian policies
that Hayek had claimed had led to the high levels of inflation in the
1970s, and her government no longer increased the supply of money
in an effort to induce economic activity. Perhaps most significantly,
it also accepted unemployment as a necessary short-term evil. Her
administration sold off state-owned businesses, diminished direct government intervention in the economy, encouraged entrepreneurship
and reduced taxes. By the time she left office in 1990, Thatcher had
presided over the structural transformation of the British economy,

and perhaps the greatest triumph of Thatcherism was in so transform-
ing British politics that many of her policies and much of her rhetoric
were copied by the Labour Party under Tony Blair.[29]

On the other side of the Atlantic Hayek also had a significant influence upon the policy orientation of the Presidency of Ronald Reagan.
Of Reagan's 74 economic advisors during his 1980 election campaign,
20 were members of the Mt. Pèlerin Society that Hayek had founded
almost 25 years before.[30] Like Thatcher, Reagan was also prepared to
tolerate unemployment, sought to curb union power, encourage entrepreneurship, cut taxes and reduce government regulation. Finally, and
similar to the effect of Thatcher upon the Labour party, Hayek's greatest long-term influence came in the transformation of the Democratic
Party under President Clinton towards views more amenable to the
market. Thus, '[f]rom a position of great isolation and apparent irrelevance in the 1940s', writes Gamble, Hayek 'found himself thirty years
later the acknowledged leader of the new political orthodoxy, the intellectual guide of prime ministers and presidents, the icon of a rapidly
growing worldwide political movement and the recipient of numerous
honours including the Nobel Prize for Economics and the Companion
of Honour'.[31]

Influence on the Wane?

Post-socialism and the cultural turn

Undoubtedly, Hayek has had a considerable influence both in the
world of ideas and in the world of politics and policy. Yet, despite this,
the collapse of communism and the retreat of the welfare state, there
are at least two reasons why it may be fair to claim today that Hayek's
influence is on the wane. Paradoxically, these are reasons that relate
directly to those historical events with which Hayek's name is often
associated. In the first instance, at least since the 1960s with the emergence of new left social movements, but also since the 1980s with the
advent of increasingly multicultural societies, Hayek's almost exclusive
concern with issues pertaining to economics and distributive justice
makes his thought seem somewhat old-fashioned.

Democratic theorist John Dryzek, for example, locates the contemporary political concern with culture in the post-communist crisis of the left, in which the prospects for a radical redistribution of

wealth were severely diminished. In the wake of what has come to be called 'the cultural turn' multiculturalism has become the principal rival to liberalism.[32] Similarly, David Miller, who understands this shift in more catholic terms as a political concern with national as well as minority identities, also links it to the collapse of communism and to a relative lessening of the attention given to issues of economic distribution. In the wake of the falling of the Berlin Wall, he writes, '[i]t matters less whether the state embraces the free market, or a planned economy, or something in between'. Rather, '[i]t matters more where the boundaries of the state are drawn, who gets included and who gets excluded, what language is used, what religion endorsed, what culture promoted'.[33] In his book *Culture and Equality* Brian Barry has claimed that the cultural turn can be traced to the demise of communism in the late 1980's and the political vacuum created by its departure.[34] In the countries where central planning failed there has arisen the often-ugly politics of ethnic nationalism. Moreover, in the West what Nancy Fraser has called the 'postsocialist' age has also witnessed the emergence of multiculturalism, or the politics of recognition.[35] This politics, as Fraser and Iris Marion Young have pointed out, has often taken inspiration from the New Social Movements of the left; those grassroots political movements that arose in the 1960s and 1970s in defence of the claims of, among others, women, gays and ethnic and national minorities, which gained further momentum with the collapse of communism.[36] Finally, in the liberal democracies of the West, the cultural turn has also been manifested in an upsurge in nationalist discourses that, particularly since 9/11, are sharply critical of multiculturalism and of the politics of difference.[37]

In academic political philosophy these developments have been reflected in the increased attention devoted to issues of culture and identity in the theory of justice. Indeed, their significance can be seen in the fact that many, if not most, political theorists accept as a starting point for discussion of these issues what has come to be called, following Rawls, the fact of pluralism; the fact that liberal democratic societies are and always stand to be marked by a diversity of conceptions of the good, each competing for the attention of the body politic and the benefits and burdens it confers.[38] Developments in liberal political theory in particular reflect this in the emergence of John Rawls' 'political liberal' approaches to the justification of liberal institutions. Thus, despite their clear differences, theorists as diverse as Rawls,

Will Kymlicka, Young and Miller all work from the assumption of the importance of culture and identity to politics.

The problem, then, is that there appears to be little scope for a Hayekian contribution to contemporary political philosophy, precisely because it now finds itself in a postsocialist age that, to the extent that it is concerned with economic questions at all, is in any case less concerned with them relative to its concern with questions pertaining to culture, identity and difference. It is right, then, to consider Hayek as not only working from within Young's 'distributive paradigm' but to be one of its archetypal representatives.[39] His is a perspective that may have something of interest to say about economic management in Soviet Russia, or the distributive implications of Rawls's Difference Principle, but must remain silent, upon pain of irrelevance, on issues such as female circumcision, gay marriage, discrimination or the political significance of national identity. Indeed, as John Gray has claimed, by deploying such important epistemological arguments against centralized economic planning that simultaneously offer powerful explanations for recent developments in politics and political theory, far from placing him centre-stage in the post-socialist world, Hayek has become one of the principal historical victims of those arguments' persuasiveness.[40]

Another major difficulty for Hayek relates not to the distributive focus of his research project but rather to its epistemological basis. In his study, *Hayek's Social and Political Thought*, Roland Kley distinguishes Hayek from other recent Anglo-American political philosophers in one very fundamental respect. Theorists such as Rawls, Ronald Dworkin, Joseph Raz and David Gauthier, 'seek primarily to work out the foundations of liberal political morality and to justify on moral grounds liberalism's overriding concerns'.[41] Unlike Hayek, he continues, such theorists do not consider political disagreement to be 'merely about the institutional means to universally shared ends but in the very ends and values themselves to which legitimate government must be committed'.[42] As we have seen, Hayek was not in the main concerned with moral argument at all when he sought to justify liberal institutions.

This view marks Hayek off sharply from the mainstream for whom, at least since *A Theory of Justice*, 'moral justification has quickly become the dominant paradigm of what political philosophy is all about'.[43] If true, and as we discussed with reference to his legal theory, Kley's reading has very serious implications for the contemporary status of Hayekian liberalism and makes Gray's argument about the historical marginality of Hayekian political theory discussed earlier still more relevant. For the amoral, instrumental nature of Hayek's normative enterprise means that, despite the historical significance of the distributive arguments he did make, his political theory is necessarily an incomplete one because it lacks the very moral argumentation needed either to engage with issues of culture and identity, or with debates about the proper scope of markets and the domain of individual liberty.[44] Thus, Hayek's epistemological liberalism has been rendered largely tangential to contemporary concerns by the historical confirmation of some of its core distributive insights. One may also add that it does not, in any case, possess the requisite philosophical resources to reconnect itself to those mainstream postsocialist research programmes that have arisen since the collapse of communism. In the present context, then, the veracity of the claim that Hayek's is an amoral, instrumental project means that the prospects for a postsocialist epistemological account of justice appear decidedly gloomy. Hayek's irrelevance is not only historical in character. It is an irredeemably philosophical irrelevance.

Social justice

The second sense in which Hayek's political thought may find itself in an increasingly tangential position with regard to mainstream concerns draws on Gray's claim that, even if he is able to provide a general case for markets, Hayek cannot tell us precisely where to draw their boundaries. Yet, in an age where central planning is no longer seriously defended, answers to such questions are needed if we are to address the issues of poverty and economic inequality that underlay the desire to control the outcomes of the market process. That Hayek did not provide a specific classical liberal response to the issue of economic inequality raises a third problem with his treatment of social justice. Significantly, Hayek's position is that he not only dismisses social justice but actually describes the inequalities it is intended to address as socially necessary.[45] To the extent that the issue of economic inequality does feature in his political thought at all, it does so merely as part of a wider description of the catallactic process being one which needs to allow for economic failure in order for society as a whole to learn what should and, importantly, should *not* be done. Central here is Hayek's idea of the economic process not only being one of wealth-creation but also of imitative learning in which individuals, organizations and society as a whole learn how to improve things they are already doing well and to terminate activities that are of no perceived benefit to others. In brief, then, in the catallactic process we learn to which enterprises we should *not* be directing our efforts as much as we learn about those to which we should and it is in this sense that the market functions properly 'at the price of a constant disappointment of some expectations'.[46] Thus, Hayek claims that

> [i]t is one of the chief reasons for the dislike of competition that it not only shows how things may be done more effectively, but also confronts those who depend for their incomes on the market with the alternative of imitating the more successful or losing some or all of their income.[47]

That is, in order for knowledge of material needs and availabilities to be properly coordinated so that resources are devoted to their most productive use, there must be room for the transmission of the 'negative feedback' of economic failure and the harsh personal consequences that come with it.[48]

This reality ties in directly with Hayek's worry about the enduring attractiveness of the idea of social justice and of our unwillingness to accept a form of economic decision-making the aggregate results of which, if we are to accept his critique, cannot be meaningfully said to be just or unjust.[49] As Irving Kristol and Gamble have pointed out, however, the very survival of the market order is at risk unless the members of society believe 'that the distribution of wealth that it produces is just'.[50] In other words, unless we believe, erroneously according to Hayek, that there is such a thing as social justice that can be predicated of catallactic outcomes it seems difficult to see how political allegiance to it is sustainable. Thus, there is a major problem, if not for the plausibility, then for the *palatability* and *sustainability* of Hayek's classical liberalism. Not only is the idea of social justice a reactionary, unachievable illusion whose inevitably unsuccessful pursuit will do more harm than good, the very economic inequality it seeks to mitigate is, according to Hayek, actually a socially necessary phenomenon without which no recognizable market order can properly function. If this is so there seems to be no realistic chance of that theory ever being fully implemented a problem which, whilst curiously not discussing it at length, Feser considers to be 'the most serious and important of the objections made to Hayek's position'.[51] The key question for Hayek on social justice is not whether he failed to give a response to the question of the poor in a market society after having rejected social justice; in Chapter 5, the textual evidence clearly shows that he did. Rather the problem is that the response he gave was not only incompatible with his critiques but wholly incompatible with the philosophical underpinnings of the epistemological liberal approach that informs them.

Contemporary Relevance

Hayek and the epistemological significance of culture

What, then, of the relevance of Hayek's thought today? To assess the extent to which, if at all, Hayek's thought resonates with contemporary concerns, we will look at issues which command significant attention: the implications of cultural diversity for social and political organization, and the enduring preoccupation with social justice. More specifically, despite what appear to be the serious theoretical obstacles discussed in the previous chapter, Hayek's thought nonetheless continues to be relevant, not least because it offers such an original and fruitful way of thinking about these issues.

There are at least two senses in which this apparently 'distributivist' perspective is relevant to the just resolution of contemporary controversies in diverse complex societies. Central to the first sense is the Hayekian account of the circumstances of justice described in Chapter 4. Regarding the economic organization of society, it was because of the circumstance identified by the Knowledge Problem that Hayek claimed that the task of economic justice was not to attempt to determine the specifics of the catallactic process, but rather to cultivate and enforce a legal regime that devolved to individuals and voluntary associations of them authoritative decision-making about economic matters. Importantly, however, and despite endorsing the market in this manner, Hayek's political theory should not be read in narrow terms as only being concerned with individuals' economic activities. Firstly, this is because there ultimately are no purely economic actions, as these are merely the means by which we reconcile our diverse purposes, very few of which are ultimately economic.[52] In addition, his account of the market as a discovery procedure not only pertains to the discovery of information concerning the cost, scarcity, or optimal distribution of resources, but also to social and cultural questions. For Hayek, that is, the market is also to be understood as facilitating the discovery of precisely what things are to count as goods and how scarce and valuable they are.[53] As Kukathas has claimed the Knowledge Problem at the heart of Hayek's research project

> characterizes not simply the production process but the human condition generally. The market, defined by the institutions of justice, is to be praised not merely for making production cheaper; for what is discovered in the market is not simply 'economic' knowledge, but knowledge of the world, of others, and even of oneself.[54]

Perhaps most importantly, however, the underlying logic of Hayek's arguments for individual economic liberty are also significant insofar as they relate to issues of culture and identity in complex modern societies. Like many thinkers at the time he theorized justice with an underlying assumption of cultural homogeneity; Hayek never addressed the issue of how the coordination problem would be affected if the rules we follow were themselves different to one another as they are in culturally diverse societies. Thus, developing a cultural variant of the Hayekian argument, we may claim that the human condition is not only marked by an economic coordination problem, but also by a similar problem with respect to the very rules, traditions and practices which facilitate that coordination. Of special importance here is the fact that in a culturally diverse society, these coordinating rules, traditions and practices may recommend that we do entirely different and possibly conflicting things under identical social circumstances, thus undermining the social coordination they are supposed to make possible. An example of this problem is when different conceptions of decency conflict, for instance, when one tradition considers the wearing of a *niqab* or a *burkha* to be an offensive sexist and degrading practice that should be banned, whilst another requires women to wear them precisely on grounds of modesty, piety and public decency. The important political question then becomes which of these two norms governing public decency should take precedence in society as a whole so that social coordination can take place? Typically, what is in effect a cultural coordination problem not within, but *between* traditions, is resolved centrally in a legislature or a court. Here, arguments are heard for a ban on the practice concerned, or for legal protections for those who follow it, with the resulting decision being binding upon all.

In opposition to this approach, the Hayekian response would commence with the claim that, just as it is resistant to centralization in the economic domain, the knowledge of the factors relevant to deciding this matter in an equitable way is uncentralizable, with the consequence that any decision reached would be bound to be an inadequate one. In the first instance, this is because, as the embodiment of past experience accumulated in response to specific circumstances to which no single mind could have access, the reasons why a particular practice has value are resistant to the conscious articulation which is the hallmark of centralized decision-making. More importantly still, all the circumstances that give rise to and determine the future appropriateness of rules and practices are also situational and constantly changing, again defeating the possibility that they could adequately figure as reasons in any centralized political resolution of a conflict between norms. Thus, in a complex society, the vast majority of the considerations relevant to deciding whether the *burkha* should be banned or whether those who choose for moral reasons to wear it should enjoy legal protections from those who, for their own moral reasons disapprove, are not available to a central authority such as a legislature. Finally, to the extent that we can articulate them at all, the reasons we have for believing why a particular practice should or should not be acceptable can only ever come from within the confines of our own inherited body of moral rules. But these rules are themselves only reflective of the circumstances relevant to their emergence and not to those of the community whose practice with which we disagree. Clearly, then, it would be nonsensical to appeal to a particular body of rules, traditions and practices as the appropriate ethical reference point for deciding a conflict *between* the traditions of different communities. Given this problem, an account is needed that explains how a resolution of the conflict can take into consideration all the relevant circumstances.

Hayekian liberalism is unique, therefore, in claiming that the important political issue is not the fact of disagreement, or the *plurality* of opinion about the good life. These are, ultimately, only symptomatic of a deeper problem. Rather, it is the underlying *epistemological* problem of how society can make use of the tacit, dispersed and fleeting knowledge of the circumstances relevant to deciding how its members should coordinate their action. The principal task of justice with respect to culture and identity is not for public institutions to enforce a particular conception of the good life, nor a culturally specific ethical ideal about what the consequences of adherence to diverse norms should be. Rather, it is to provide institutions that secure the utilization of the knowledge relevant to the discovery of answers to these important questions under ever-changing social circumstances.

A cultural discovery process or a politics of culture?

Hayek's epistemological account of the circumstances of justice and the cultural coordination problem it points to gives rise to the second sense in which his perspective is relevant to contemporary debates about justice, culture and identity. Central here is the importance he attaches to the role cultural evolution plays as a mechanism for deciding which rules and norms are adopted by a society. As the example of public decency shows, no longer does cultural evolution have to be understood in Hayek's own terms as a norm selection process within a single culture. Rather, it may be glossed to refer to the competition for adherents that occurs within societies between sometimes conflicting norms. Importantly, and consistent with Hayek's account, the very process of individual approval, disapproval and imitative learning that lies at the heart of the theory of cultural evolution is the process by which rules and traditions are transformed. Thus, answers to questions about which specific rules and traditions ought to be followed and the consequences of doing so are not given via a centralized process of political decision-making. Rather, they are answered as part of a wider cumulative and largely imitative process whose outcome is the result of the decisions of disparate and mutually ignorant individuals.

Such a liberalism should not result in a cultural *carte blanche* where individuals and groups could do as they wished to one another – and particularly to children and others considered incapable of consent – in the name of 'their culture'. Precisely because the knowledge relevant to the process is only ever located within individual minds, it would be grounded in an epistemologically derived commitment to individual freedom and equality that was itself strictly neutral between different conceptions of the good. That is, for the Hayekian liberal, individual freedom is not valued because it alone is capable of serving as the foundation for a political *morality*, nor because it is the political value which best satisfies the aspirations of our universally shared ethical commitments; it is to be valued on epistemological grounds because it 'is the source and condition of most values' and, additionally, the political commitment we must share in order for decisions on which rules, traditions and practices ought to be adopted by society as a whole.[55]

This Hayekian defence of liberal individualism as the framework for the cultural evolution rather than the political selection of rules provides the basis for some important critiques of the major contemporary responses to diversity. Central to identity-based theories of justice such as multiculturalism and nationalism is a misrecognition of society's cultural coordination problem that results in a misconception of the very task of justice with respect to culture and identity. Rather than defend an account of justice that facilitates the *discovery* of what the relative status of diverse identities and of the rules and practices they endorse should be, both schools assume that this issue has already been resolved. With respect to multiculturalism this much is clear in its defence of public institutions that seek to insulate minority identities and practices from the arbitration of the wider cultural process via, for example, regimes of cultural rights and, with respect to some matters, anti-discrimination legislation. A logically similar phenomenon occurs in nationalism's defence of immigration controls and cultural assimilation in social and educational policy, or as is sometimes somewhat narrowly called 'Anglo-conformity'.[56] In both cases, the consequence of this misrecognition is a failure to be properly sensitive to the epistemological burdens that come with membership.

The knowledge problem and social justice

Regardless of what may or may not be said from a Hayekian perspective about culture and identity, Hayek's writings on social justice reveal a deep inconsistency in his thought that warrants the claim that his engagement with the question of the proper response of the state to economic inequality fails. This failure, moreover, is deeply significant for the future prospects of Hayekian political theory. Despite the important pro-market reforms of the last generation, of which Hayek undoubtedly would have approved, the moral concerns that animate social justice endure and will continue to do so. A proper Hayekian response to social justice, then, is as important today as it was in Hayek's time. Similarly to its centrality with regard to culture and identity, Hayek's account of the epistemological circumstances of justice provides the foundation for a Hayekian reengagement with social justice, which opens up a new path both in Hayek scholarship and in the debate about the requirements of social justice. It is the option of retracting Hayek's ill-considered safety net concession and replacing it with a positive response to economic inequality that is consistent with the fundamental epistemological presuppositions of his liberalism. Moreover, these are arguments that support the claim that the kinds of classical liberal institutions Hayek defended, rather than those of the liberal welfare state, would be best suited to ameliorate the position of the least well-off in a modern complex society.

Two of the central themes from Hayek's *corpus* are relevant to this option: the universal nature of his Knowledge Problem and the state's cultivation – but not the direction – of the economic circumstances of society. The claim about the irremediably diffuse, fleeting and tacit nature of social knowledge in complex modern societies and the fact that it can never be concentrated in its totality in a single mind was the starting point for Hayek's research project that sought to explain how liberal institutions nonetheless communicate it. Importantly precisely because the knowledge problem ultimately says something significant about the social constitution of reason, it is equally applicable regard-less of the kinds of goods or services under consideration. These may range from traditionally understood goods and services such as food, motorcars and banking, but can also include the devoting of resources to the least well-off. Whatever it is that one seeks to provide, from a Hayekian perspective, the institutional basis of that provision must reflect the fact that all the knowledge necessary to do so effec-tively is never given to any single agent but is only ever recoverable by institutions that allow that knowledge to be effectively utilized and communicated.

Of course, this Hayekian account accepts that the pursuit of social justice is only one objective among many that we may be concerned to pursue with resources. For this reason, poverty alleviation can only ever take its place among many other pursuits and should not be consid-ered a social good that trumps all others. There is no formal commit-ment to direct state provision of an economic minimum, not because such a minimum may not exist but because, in the first instance, in a world of scarce resources and ever-changing circumstances, it may not be sustainable and, in the second, because knowledge of those circum-stances is never given in its totality. Of course, once these qualifications are accepted, the appropriate criterion in virtue of which alternative institutional responses by the state to economic inequality changes con-siderably. To argue from the assumption that the resources potentially at disposal for the pursuit of social justice are unlimited, and that all the knowledge relevant to achieving a socially just outcome is already available would, on this reading, be to argue from a standpoint that has no bearing whatsoever on the human condition. It is for these reasons that a consistently pursued Hayekian approach would claim that, rather than directly provide a minimum itself, the State should devolve the discovery and implementation of appropriate responses to poverty and economic inequality to individuals and voluntary associations of them.

To the attempt to ensure an adequate baseline of material well-being below which nobody will fall, this means that, just as with economic coordination in general, the task of social justice is reformulated from being a question about how a pre-determined minimum should be achieved to one that asks: *which institutions of justice ensure the most efficacious determination and provision of an adequate baseline of material well-being under conditions of limited resources and dispersed, fleeting and tacit knowledge?* This general question presupposes at least two other questions, both of which are subject to the strictures of Hayek's epistemological problematic. Firstly, what is the appropriate baseline of material well-being and, secondly, how to pursue it? In both cases the fact that the knowledge of the circumstances relevant to the determination of the answer is dispersed, fleeting and tacit in nature means that answers to these questions need to be discovered rather than assumed to be already self-evident. On the Hayekian reading the epistemological problem faced by society means that it is better to devolve authoritative decision-making about raising the situation of the least well-off to individuals and organized groups of them, because it is only within individual minds that the relevant knowledge of local conditions and needs is located. Thus, by decentralizing decision-making to individuals and groups in this way, society's stock of knowledge relevant to poverty alleviation can be as fully exploited as possible.

This knowledge is not only that relevant to the fulfilment of the most obvious and immediate strategies for economic uplift such as charitable-giving and insurance but also to those yet-to-be-discovered, such as was the case with microfinance and microcredit a generation ago. Importantly, then, the whole rationale behind the Hayekian approach is that strategies are constantly being devised in response to the ever-changing causes and circumstances of poverty. This Hayekian approach to social justice also involves emphasising the importance of the twin ideas of competition and negative feedback. Importantly, however, their role would be in contrast to the somewhat chilling one they play in Hayek's own account of the market. On that account, we saw that competition and negative feedback could be seen to function essentially as euphemisms for personal economic failure, from which individuals and society as a whole nonetheless learn of the purposes to which resources should and should not be devoted. In contrast, for poverty alleviation the ideas of competition and negative feedback refer to the social discovery, via a process of imitative learning, of new and innovative ways of ameliorating the position of the least well-off. As such, these notions assume a crucial role in the process of how a society learns which methods are most and least effective. Indeed the exploitation of the unequal results yielded by employing differing approaches to poverty alleviation is precisely how the catallactic discovery process that Hayek's theory describes gains an advantage over more centralized approaches. This is so not least because the rejection of methods that have been shown to be ineffective as correctives to economic inequality and poverty is of vital importance if our goal is to help the least well-off under the conditions stipulated by the Hayekian account of the circumstances of justice.

Cultivating the circumstances of socially just outcomes

This Hayekian account of poverty alleviation relates in two respects to the second theme that is central to Hayek's research project: the role of the state in the self-conscious cultivation of the circumstances conducive to the utilization of knowledge in a complex society. Firstly, the state assumes an indispensable role in the enforcement of the rules of just conduct that makes the utilization of the dispersed, fleeting and tacit knowledge that is necessary for the pursuit of social justice possible where these rules are not honoured in action. Secondly, the theme of the state as cultivator rather than director of the economic circumstances of society relates directly to Hayek's account of the socially efficacious use of conscious reason. Importantly, and similar to his account of the role of conscious reason in his theory of spontaneous order in general, and of the market or *catallaxy* in particular, adopting a stance of cultivation rather than direction towards the alleviation of poverty and the reduction of economic inequality is something we, as a political society, can undertake quite deliberately. With a theory such as Hayek's, which describes the beneficial consequences of the operation of liberal economic institutions, we in turn as citizens, public office-holders and policy-makers can self-consciously elect to adopt them. We do so, moreover, in the knowledge that this will lead to socially beneficial outcomes with respect to poverty alleviation relative to any other set of institutions, given the epistemological circumstances of justice that the theory selects as of primary importance.

The moral is that understanding what can and cannot be achieved by conscious reason in a complex society is itself an exercise of the power of reason, and does not assume or result in blind capitulation to the forces Hayek describes in his theory of spontaneous social order. Indeed, we may use the theory of spontaneous order precisely to make conscious political decisions that enable us to harness its power. The central message of any future Hayekian engagement with the concerns of social justice, then, is that to do this much, and in this way, is entirely appropriate given the epistemological circumstances of modern complex societies. From this perspective, adopting pre-political libertarian rights in order to defend a robust economic liberalism is not required. Nor, perhaps contrary to what Hayek himself thought, is it necessary to defend direct state provision of an economic minimum. In a complex society, to attempt to do more than cultivate the circumstances conducive to the alleviation of poverty would in an important sense be to end up doing *less* rather than more and run the risk of fatally underusing the most valuable resource in combating poverty, economic inequality and the sources of both.

What, then, are we to make of Hayek's thought in the new millennium, given that the question of which institutional arrangements best respond to cultural diversity and economic inequality under the epistemological circumstances of justice is one to which it would seem to be able to offer insightful answers? Clearly, the two research projects of which we have offered only an outline here were, for various reasons, never embarked upon by Hayek himself. In the case of the politics of culture and identity, and despite clearly emphasizing culture in his own research project, Hayek could perhaps be excused, because he wrote largely at a time that was more preoccupied with questions of just distribution. With respect to poverty alleviation and the reduction of economic inequality, the omission is perhaps surprising, not least given the universal nature of the Knowledge Problem that always occupied such a prominent place in his multidisciplinary output. That he did not do so also means that the dawning of an ever more complex, 'postsocialist' age will probably not be followed by the twilight of Hayekian political theory.

Notes

[1] The Sveriges Riksbank Prize in Economic Sciences in Memory of Alfred Nobel 1974, The Nobel Foundation, 1974.

[2] Myrdal is reported to have said that, had he known he would be sharing the prize with Hayek he would not have accepted it and indeed later suggested that the prize be done away with altogether, given that it had been awarded to Hayek and Milton Friedman. Ebenstein, A., *Friedrich Hayek: A Biography*, Chicago, IL, University of Chicago Press, (2001) 2003, p. 261.

[3] Ebenstein, A., *Hayek's Journey: The Mind of Friedrich Hayek*, New York, Palgrave MacmIllan, 2003, p. 90; Gamble, *Hayek: The Iron Cage of Liberty*, Boulder, CO, Westview Press, 1996, p. 152.

[4] Keynes, J. M., *A Treatise on Money*, 2 vols., London, MacMillan, 1930.

[5] Skidelsky, R., 'Hayek versus Keynes: The Road to Reconciliation', in Feser, E. (ed.), *The Cambridge Companion to Hayek*, Cambridge, Cambridge University Press, 2006, pp. 82–110.

[6] For Hayek's review see his 'Reflections on *The Pure Theory of Money* of Mr. J. M. Keynes', in Hayek, F. A. (ed.), *Prices and Production and Other Works: F. A. Hayek On Money, the Business Cycle and the Gold Standard*, Auburn, AL, The Ludwig von Mises Institute, (1931/1932) 2008, pp. 423–485.

[7] Keynes, J. M., *General Theory of Employment, Money and Interest*, London, MacMillan, 1936.

[8] Caldwell, B., *Hayek's Challenge: An Intellectual Biography of F. A. Hayek*, Chicago, IL, University of Chicago Press, 2004, p. 175.

[9] Gamble, Hayek: *The Iron Cage of Liberty*, p. 153.

[10] Hayek, *Hayek on Hayek: An Autobiographical Dialogue*, in Kresge, S. and Wenar, L. (eds), London, Routledge, 1994, pp. 90–91.

[11] Ebenstein, Friedrich Hayek: A Biography, pp. 72–73; Gamble, *Hayek: The Iron Cage of Liberty*, p. 152.

[12] Useful summaries of this is given by Vaughn, K., 'The Mengerian Roots of the Austrian Revival', in Caldwell, B. (ed.), *Carl Menger and his Legacy in Economics*, Durham, Duke University Press, 1990, pp. 379–407, esp. pp. 388–395 and Steele, G. R., *The Economics of Friedrich Hayek*, Basingstoke, Palgrave MacMillan, (2nd edn) 2007.

[13] Gamble, *Hayek: The Iron Cage of Liberty*, p. 153.

[14] Keynes, 'Letter to Hayek , 28 June, 1944', in Keynes, J. M. (ed.), *The Collected Writings of John Maynard Keynes*, London, MacmIllan, 1980, p. 385.

[15] Orwell, G., *The Collected Essays Journalism and Letters of George Orwell*, vol. 3, Orwell, S. And Angus, I. (eds), New York, Harcourt, Brace and World, 1968, p. 119.

[16] Ebenstein, *Friedrich Hayek: A Biography*, pp. 128–134.

[17] Orwell, G., op cit.

[18] Finer, H., *The Road to Reaction*, Boston, MA, Little Brown and Co., 1945, p. xii; Caldwell, B.,*Hayek's Challenge*, p. 148, n. 19.

[19] Wootton, B., *Freedom under Planning*, London, George Allen and Unwin, 1945, p. 5.

[20] Hayek, *Hayek on Hayek*, pp. 24–25, 152–153. *The Road to Serfdom*, Chicago, IL, University of Chicago Press, (1944) 1976, p. xxi.

[21] Keynes, 'Letter to Hayek , 28 June, 1944', p. 386.

[22] Sydney Hook quoted in Ebenstein, *Friedrich Hayek: A Biography*, p. 203; Quinton, A., 'Introduction', in Quinton, A. (ed.), *Political Philosophy*, Oxford, Oxford University Press, 1967, p. 2.

[23] Robbins, L., 'Hayek on Liberty', *Economica*, February 1961, pp. 66–81; Viner, J., 'Hayek on Freedom and Coercion', *Southern Economic Journal*, vol. 27, January 1961, pp. 230–236; Knight, F. 'Laissez Faire: Pro and Con', *Journal of Political Economy*, vol. 75, October 1967, pp. 782–795; Hamowy, R., 'Hayek's Concept of Freedom: A Critique', *New Individualist Review*, April, 1961, pp. 28–31.

[24] Quoted in Ebenstein, *Hayek's Journey: The Mind of Friedrich Hayek*, p. 184.

[25] Quoted in Ebenstein, *Friedrich Hayek: A Biography*, p. 138. See also Gamble, *Hayek: The Iron Cage of Liberty*, pp. 77–78.

[26] Cockett, R., *Thinking the Unthinkable: Think-Tanks and the Economic Counter-Revolution 1931–1983*, New York, Harper Collins, 1995, p. 174.

[27] *The Daily Telegraph*, London, 14 May 1978 quoted in Ebenstein, A., *Friedrich Hayek: A Biography*, p. 293.

[28] Hayek, F. A., *1980s Unemployment and the Unions*, London, Institute of Economic Affairs, (1980) 1984.

[29] Muller, *The Mind and the Market: Capitalism in Western Thought*, New York, Anchor Books, 2002, p. 381.

[30] Ibid., p. 382.

[31] Gamble, *Hayek: The Iron Cage of Liberty*, p. 10; Ebenstein, Friedrich Hayek: A Biography, pp. 207–209.

[32] Dryzek, J., *Deliberative Democracy and Beyond: Liberals, Critics, Contestations*, Oxford, Oxford University Press, 2000, p. 57.

[33] Miller, D., *On Nationality*, Oxford, Oxford University Press, 1995, p. 1.

[34] Barry, B., *Culture and Equality*, Oxford, Polity Press, 2000, pp. 3–5.

[35] Fraser, N., 'From Redistribution to Recognition? Dilemmas of Justice in a "Postsocialist" Age' in Fraser, N. (ed.), *Justice Interruptus: Critical Reflections on the "Postsocialist" Condition*, New York, Routledge, 1996, pp. 11–39.

[36] As such, multiculturalism should be construed in broad terms that comprehend but are not exhausted by specifically cultural claims. Young, I. M., *Justice and the Politics of Difference*, Princeton, NJ, Princeton University Press, 1990.

[37] Tebble, A. J., 'Exclusion for Democracy', *Political Theory*, vol. 34, no. 4, 2006, 463–487.

[38] Rawls, J., *Political Liberalism*, Columbia, NY, Columbia University Press, 1993, pp. xviii–ixx.

[39] Young, I. M., *Justice and the Politics of Difference*, pp. 15–19.

[40] Gray, J., *Hayek on Liberty*, London, Routledge, 3rd edn, (1984) 1998, pp. 146–161.

[41] Kley, *Hayek's Social and Political Thought*, Oxford, Clarendon Press, 1994, p. 12.

[42] Ibid. See also Sandel, *Liberalism and the Limits of Justice*, Cambridge, Cambridge University Press, 1982, pp. 175–178.

[43] Ibid., p. 11.

[44] Gray, *Hayek on Liberty*, pp. 146–161.

[45] Hayek, *The Mirage of Social Justice*, London, Routledge, 1976a, pp. 71, 94, 107–132.

[46] Ibid., p. 107, pp. 124–128. See also Hayek, *Rules and Order*, London, Routledge, 1973, pp. 102–106.

[47] Hayek, 'Competition as a Discovery Procedure', *The Quarterly Journal of Austrian Economics*, vol. 5, no. 3, (1968b) 2002, p. 19.

[48] Hayek, *The Mirage of Social Justice*, p. 94.

[49] Ibid., pp. 65–67.

[50] Kristol, I., 'Capitalism, Socialism, and Nihilism', in Kirk, R., (ed.), *The Portable Conservative Reader*. New York, Viking, 1982, pp. 627–643 and Gamble, *Hayek: The Iron Cage of Liberty*, p. 49.

[51] Feser, 'Hayek on Social Justice: Reply to Lukes and Johnston' , *Critical Review*, vol. 11, no. 4 (Fall 1997), p. 602.

[52] Hayek, *The Constitution of Liberty*, London, Routledge, 1960, p. 35.

[53] Hayek, 'Competition as a Discovery Procedure', p. 13.

[54] Kukathas, *Hayek and Modern Liberalism*, Oxford, Clarendon Press, 1989, p. 101.

[55] Hayek, *The Constitution of Liberty*, p. 6.

[56] Scruton, R., *The Meaning of Conservatism*, London, MacMillan, 1980; In Defence of the Nation', in Scruton, R. (ed.), *The Philosopher on Dover Beach*, London, St. Martin's Press, 1990, pp. 299–328; 'The First Person Plural', in Beiner, R. (ed.) *Theorizing Nationalism*, New York, SUNY Press, 1999, pp. 279–293. Kymlicka, W., *Multicultural Citizenship: A Liberal Theory of Minority Rights*, Oxford, Oxford University Press, 1995, pp. 14–15.

Bibliography

Ayer, A. J., *The Problem of Knowledge*, London, MacMillan, 1956.

Barry, B., *Culture and Equality*, Oxford, Polity Press, 2000.

—, *Why Social Justice Matters*, Cambridge, Polity Press, 2005.

Baumgarth, W. P., 'Hayek and Political Order: The Rule of Law', *Journal of Libertarian Studies*, vol. 2, no. 1, 1978, pp. 11–28.

Bellamy, R., *Liberalism and Pluralism: Towards a Politics of Compromise*, London, Routledge, 1999.

Boettke, P. J., 'Hayek and Market Socialism', in Feser, E. (ed.), *The Cambridge Companion to Hayek*, Cambridge, Cambridge University Press, 2006, pp. 51–66.

Burczak, T., *Socialism after Hayek*, Ann Arbor, University of Michigan Press, 2006.

Butler, J., *Giving an Account of Oneself*, New York, Fordham University Press, 2005.

Caldwell, B., *Hayek's Challenge: An Intellectual Biography of F. A. Hayek*, Chicago, University of Chicago Press, 2004.

Cockett, R., *Thinking the Unthinkable: Think-Tanks and the Economic Counter-Revolution 1931–1983*, New York, Harper Collins, 1995.

Constitution of Massachusetts, Part I, article XXX (1780).

Crossley, N., *Intersubjectivity: The Fabric of Social Becoming*, London, Sage Publications, 1996.

Daniel, N., 'Equal Liberty and Unequal Worth of Liberty', in Daniel, N. (ed.), *Reading Rawls: Critical Studies of 'A Theory of Justice'*, New York, Basic Books, 1975, pp. 253–281.

Dietze, G., 'Hayek on the Rule of Law', in Machlup, F. (ed.), *Essays on Hayek*, Hillsdale, Hillsdale College Press, 1976, pp. 107–146.

Dryzek, J., *Deliberative Democracy and Beyond: Liberals, Critics, Contestations*, Oxford, Oxford University Press, 2000.

Ebenstein, A., *Friedrich Hayek: A Biography*, Chicago, University of Chicago Press, (2001) 2003.

—, *Hayek's Journey: The Mind of Friedrich Hayek*, New York, Palgrave, 2003.

Edelman, G., 'Through a Computer Darkly: Group Selection and Higher Brain Function', *Bulletin of the American Academy of Arts and Sciences*, vol. 36, no. 1, 1982, pp. 20–49.

Feser, E., 'Hayek on Social Justice: Reply to Lukes and Johnston', *Critical Review*, vol. 11, no. 4 (Fall 1997), pp. 581–606.

Finer, H., *The Road to Reaction*, Boston, Little Brown and Co., 1945.

150   *Bibliography*

Fraser, N., 'From Redistribution to Recognition? Dilemmas of Justice in a "Postsocialist" Age' in Fraser, N. (ed.), *Justice Interruptus: Critical reflections on the 'Postsocialist' Condition*, New York, Routledge, 1996, pp. 11–39.

Fuster, J., *Memory in the Cerebral Cortex: An Empirical Approach to Neural Networks in the Human and Nonhuman Primate*, Cambridge, MIT Press, 1995.

—, 'Network Memory', *Trends in Neurosciences*, vol. 20, no. 10, 1997, pp. 451–459.

Galeotti, A. E., 'Individualism, Social Rules, Tradition: The Case of Friedrich A. Hayek', *Political Theory*, vol. 15, no. 2, May 1987, pp. 163–181.

Gamble, A., *Hayek: The Iron Cage of Liberty*, Boulder, Westview Press, 1996.

Gray, J., *Hayek on Liberty*, London, Routledge, 3rd edn, (1984) 1998.

Hamowy, R., 'Hayek's Concept of Freedom: A Critique', *New Individualist Review*, vol. 1, no. 1, April 1961, pp. 28–31.

Hayek, F. A., 'Beiträge zur Theorie der Entwicklung des Bewusstseins', Grete Heim (trans.), Hoover Institution, Hayek Archives, Box 92, Folder 1, 1920.

—, *Monetary Theory and the Trade Cycle*, in Salerno, J. T. (ed.), *Prices and Production and Other Works: F. A. Hayek On Money, the Business Cycle and the Gold Standard*, Auburn, The Ludwig von Mises Institute, (1929/1933) 2008, pp. 1–130.

—, 'Reflections on *The Pure Theory of Money* of Mr. J. M. Keynes', in Salerno, J.T. (ed.), *Prices and Production and Other Works: F. A. Hayek On Money, the Business Cycle and the Gold Standard*, Auburn, The Ludwig von Mises Institute, (1931/1932) 2008, pp. 423–485.

—, *Prices and Production*, in Hayek, F.A. (ed.), *Prices and Production and Other Works: F. A. Hayek On Money, the Business Cycle and the Gold Standard*, Auburn, The Ludwig von Mises Institute, (1931/1935) 2008, pp. 189–329.

—, 'The Nature and History of the Problem', in Hayek, F.A. (ed.), *Collectivist Economic Planning: Critical Studies on The Possibilities Of Socialism*, Auburn, The Ludwig von Mises Institute, (1935) 2009, pp. 1–40.

—, 'Economics and Knowledge', in Salerno, J.T. (ed.), *Individualism and Economic Order*, Chicago, University of Chicago Press, (1936) 1948, pp. 33–56.

—, *Profits, Interest and Invetsment*, Clifton, August M. Kelley, (1939) 1975.

—, 'Freedom and the Economic System', in Caldwell, B. (ed.) *Socialism and War: Essays, Documents, Reviews*, in *The Collected Works of F. A. Hayek*, vol. 10, Chicago, University of Chicago Press, (1939) 1997, pp. 189–211.

—, 'Socialist Calculation III: The Competitive "Solution"', in Hayek, F.A. (ed.), *Individualism and Economic Order*, Chicago, University of Chicago Press, (1940) 1948, pp. 181–208.

—, *The Pure Theory of Capital*, Auburn, Ludwig von Mises Institute, (1941) 2009.

—, 'The Facts of the Social Sciences', in Hayek, F.A. (ed.), *Individualism and Economic Order*, Chicago, University of Chicago Press, (1942) 1948, pp. 57–76.

—, *The Road to Serfdom*, Chicago, University of Chicago Press, (1944) 1976.

—, 'The Use of Knowledge in Society', in Hayek, F.A. (ed.), *Individualism and Economic Order*, Chicago, University of Chicago Press, (1945) 1948, pp. 77–91.

—, 'Individualism: True and False', in Hayek, F.A. (ed.), *Individualism and Economic Order*, Chicago, University of Chicago Press, (1946a) 1948, pp. 1–32.

—, 'The Meaning of Competition', in Hayek, F.A. (ed.), *Individualism and Economic Order*, Chicago, University of Chicago Press, (1946b) 1948, pp. 92–106.

—, '"Free" Enterprise and Competitive Order', in Hayek, F.A. (ed.), *Individualism and Economic Order*, Chicago, University of Chicago Press, (1947) 1948, pp. 107–118.

—, *John Stuart Mill and Harriet Taylor: Their Friendship and Subsequent Marriage*, London, Routledge and Kegan Paul, 1951.

—, *The Sensory Order: An Inquiry into the Foundations of Theoretical Psychology*, London, Routledge and Kegan Paul, 1952a.

—, *The Counter-Revolution of Science: Studies in the Abuse of Reason*, Indianapolis, Liberty Fund, 1952b.

—, 'Decline of the Rule of Law – I', *The Freeman*, April 20, 1953, pp. 518–520.

—, 'Decline of the Rule of Law – II', *The Freeman*, May 4, 1953, pp. 561–563.

—, *The Political Ideal of the Rule of Law*, Cairo, National Bank of Egypt, 1955a.

—, 'Degrees of Explanation', in Hayek, F.A. (ed.), *Studies in Philosophy, Politics and Economics*, London, Routledge and Kegan Paul, (1955b) 1967, pp. 3–21.

—, '*The Road to Serfdom* after Twelve Years', in Hayek, F.A. (ed.), *Studies in Philosophy, Politics and Economics*, London, Routledge and Kegan Paul, (1956) 1967, pp. 216–228.

—, 'What is "Social"? – What Does it Mean?', in Hayek, F.A. (ed.), *Studies in Philosophy, Politics and Economics*, London, Routledge and Kegan Paul, (1957/1961) 1967, pp. 237–247.

—, *The Constitution of Liberty*, London, Routledge, 1960.

—, 'Rules, Perception and Intelligibility', in Hayek, F.A. (ed.), *Studies in Philosophy, Politics and Economics*, London, Routledge and Kegan Paul, (1962a) 1967, pp. 43–65.

—, 'The Moral Element in Free Enterprise', in Hayek, F.A. (ed.), *Studies in Philosophy, Politics and Economics*, London, Routledge and Kegan Paul, (1962b) 1967, pp. 229–236.

—, 'The Economy, Science and Politics', in Hayek, F.A. (ed.), *Studies in Philosophy, Politics and Economics*, London, Routledge and Kegan Paul, (1963) 1967, pp. 251–269.

—, 'The Theory of Complex Phenomena', in Hayek F.A. (ed.), *Studies in Philosophy, Politics and Economics*, London, Routledge and Kegan Paul, (1964a) 1967, pp. 22–42.

—, 'The Legal and Political Philosophy of David Hume', in Hayek, F.A. (ed.), *Studies in Philosophy, Politics and Economics*, London, Routledge and Kegan Paul, (1964b) 1967, pp. 106–121.

—, 'Kinds of Rationalism', in Hayek, F.A. (ed.), *Studies in Philosophy, Politics and Economics*, London, Routledge and Kegan Paul, (1965) 1967, pp. 82–95.

—, 'The Principles of a Liberal Social Order', in Hayek, F.A. (ed.), *Studies in Philosophy, Politics and Economics*, London, Routledge and Kegan Paul, (1966) 1967, pp. 160–177.

Hayek, F. A., 'Notes on the Evolution of Systems of Rules of Conduct', in Hayek, F.A. (ed.), *Studies in Philosophy, Politics and Economics*, London, Routledge and Kegan Paul, 1967a, pp. 66–81.

—, 'The Results of Human Action but not of Human Design', in Hayek, F.A. (ed.), *Studies in Philosophy, Politics and Economics*, London, Routledge and Kegan Paul, 1967b, pp. 96–105.

—, 'The Constitution of a Liberal State', in Hayek, F.A. (ed.), *New Studies in Philosophy, Politics, Economics and the History of Ideas*, London, Routledge and Kegan Paul, (1967c) 1978, pp. 98–118.

—, 'Dr. Bernard Mandeville', in Hayek, F.A. (ed.), *New Studies in Philosophy, Politics, Economics and the History of Ideas*, London, Routledge and Kegan Paul, (1967d) 1978, pp. 249–266.

—, 'The Confusion of Language in Political Thought', in Hayek, F.A. (ed.), *New Studies in Philosophy, Politics, Economics and the History of Ideas*, London, Routledge and Kegan Paul, (1968a) 1978, pp. 90–91.

—, 'Competition as a Discovery Procedure', *The Quarterly Journal of Austrian Economics*, vol. 5, no. 3, (1968b) 2002, pp. 9–23.

—, 'The Primacy of the Abstract', in Hayek, F.A. (ed.), *New Studies in Philosophy, Politics, Economics and the History of Ideas*, London Routledge and Kegan Paul, (1969) 1978, pp. 35–49.

—, 'The Errors of Constructivism', in Hayek, F.A. (ed.), *New Studies in Philosophy, Politics, Economics and the History of Ideas*, London, Routledge and Kegan Paul, (1970) 1978, pp. 3–22.

—, 'Nature v. Nurture Once Again', in Hayek, F.A. (ed.), *New Studies in Philosophy, Politics, Economics and the History of Ideas*, London, Routledge and Kegan Paul, (1971) 1978, pp. 290–294.

—, *Rules and Order*, London, Routledge, 1973a.

—, 'Economic Freedom and Representative Government', in Hayek, F.A. (ed.), *New Studies in Philosophy, Politics, Economics and the History of Ideas*, London, Routledge and Kegan Paul, (1973b) 1978, pp. 105–118.

—, 'Liberalism', in Hayek, F.A. (ed.), *New Studies in Philosophy, Politics, Economics and the History of Ideas*, London, Routledge and Kegan Paul, (1973c) 1978, pp. 119–151.

—, 'The Pretence of Knowledge', in Hayek, F.A. (ed.), *New Studies in Philosophy, Politics, Economic and the History of Ideas*, London, Routledge and Kegan Paul, (1975) 1978, pp. 23–34.

—, *The Mirage of Social Justice*, London, Routledge, 1976a.

—, *The Denationalization of Money: An Analysis of the Theory and Practice of Concurrent Currencies*, London, Institute of Economic Affairs, (1976b) 1990.

—, 'The Atavism of Social Justice', in Hayek, F.A. (ed.), *New Studies in Philosophy, Politics, Economic and the History of Ideas*, London, Routledge and Kegan Paul, (1976c) 1978, pp. 57–68.

—, 'Whither Democracy?', in Hayek, F.A. (ed.), *New Studies in Philosophy, Politics, Economics and the History of Ideas*, London, Routledge and Kegan Paul, (1976d) 1978, pp. 152–162.

—, 'Will the Democratic Ideal Prevail?', in Hayek, F.A. (ed.), *Economic Freedom*, Cambridge, Blackwell, (1978) 1991, pp. 399–406.

—, *The Political Order of a Free People*, London, Routledge, 1979.

—, *1980s Unemployment and the Unions*, London, Institute of Economic Affairs, (1980) 1984.

—, 'Foreword', in Mises, L. (ed.), *Socialism: And Economic ad Sociological Analysis*, 1922 (1981), Indianapolis, Liberty Classics, 1981, pp. xix–xxiv.

—, *Knowledge, Evolution and Society*, London, Adam Smith Institute, 1983.

—, *Hayek on Hayek: An Autobiographical Dialogue*, in Kresge, S. and Wenar, L. (eds), London, Routledge, 1994.

Hebb, D. O., *The Organization of Behavior*, Mahwah, Laurence Erlbaum, (1949) 2002.

Hume, D., *A Treatise of Human Nature*, Oxford, Oxford University Press, (1740) 1978.

—, *Enquiry Concerning The Principles of Morals*, Oxford, Oxford University Press, (1751) 1995.

Kant, I., *The Critique of Pure Reason*, Cambridge, Cambridge University Press, (1781/1787) 1998.

Keynes, J. M., *A Treatise on Money*, 2 vols., London, MacMillan, 1930.

—, *General Theory of Employment, Money and Interest*, London, MacMillan, 1936.

—, 'Letter to Hayek , 28 June, 1944', in Keynes, J.M. (ed.), *The Collected Writings of John Maynard Keynes*, London, MacmIllan, 1980.

Kley, R., *Hayek's Social and Political Thought*, Oxford, Clarendon Press, 1994.

Klüver, H., 'Introduction', in Hayek, F.A. (ed.), *The Sensory Order: An Inquiry into the Foundations of Theoretical Psychology*, London, Routledge and Kegan Paul, 1952, pp. xv–xxii.

Knight, F., 'Laissez Faire: Pro and Con', *Journal of Political Economy*, vol. 75, October 1967, pp. 782–795.

Kristol, I., 'Capitalism, Socialism, and Nihilism', in Kirk, R. (ed.), *The Portable Conservative Reader*, New York, Viking, 1982, pp. 627–643.

Kukathas, C., *Hayek and Modern Liberalism*, Oxford, Clarendon Press, 1989.

Kymlicka, W., *Multicultural Citizenship: A Liberal Theory of Minority Rights*, Oxford, Oxford University Press, 1995.

Lavoie, D., *Rivalry and Central Planning*, Cambridge, Cambridge University Press, 1985.

Leoni, B., *Freedom and the Law*, Los Angeles, Nash Publishing, (1961) 1972.

Locke, J., *Two Treatises of Government*, Cambridge, Cambridge University Press, (1690) 2005.

Lukes, S., *Liberals and Cannibals*, London, Verso Press, 2003.

MacIntyre, A., *Whose Justice? Which Rationality?* Notre Dame, Notre Dame University Press, 1988.

Mill, J. S., *On Liberty*, Cambridge, Cambridge University Ptess, (1859) 2005.

—, *Considerations on Representative Government*, London, Everyman, (1861) 1993.

—, *An Examination of Sir William Hamilton's Philosophy*, London, Longmans, Green and Company, (1865) 1889.

Miller, D., *On Nationality*, Oxford, Oxford University Press, 1995.

Minogue, K., 'Hayek and Conservatism: Beatrice and Benedick?', in Butler, E. and Pirie, M. (eds), *Hayek on the Fabric of Human Society*, London, Adam Smith Institute, 1987, pp. 127–145.

Mises, L., 'Economic Calculation in the Socialist Commonwealth', in Hayek, F.A. (ed.), *Collectivist Economic Planning: Critical Studies on The Possibilities Of Socialism*, Auburn, AL, The Ludwig von Mises Institute, (1920) 2009, pp. 87–130.

—, *Socialism*, Indianapolis, Liberty Fund, (1922) 1981.

—, *Human Action*, Yale, Yale University Press, 1949.

Mulhall, S. and Swift, A., *Liberals and Communitarians*, 2nd edn, Oxford, Blackwell, 1996.

Muller, J., *The Mind and the Market: Capitalism in Western Thought*, New York, Anchor Books, 2002.

Nagel, E., '[Review of] Hayek, *The Counter-Revolution of Science*', *Journal of Philosophy*, vol. 49, no. 17, (August) 1952, pp. 560–565.

Nozick, R., *Anarchy, State and Utopia*, New York, Basic Books, 1974.

O'Neill, J., 'Who won the Socialist Calculation Debate', *History of Political Thought*, vol. XVII, no. 3, Autumn 1996, pp. 431–442.

—, *The Market: Ethics, Knowledge and Politics*, London, Routledge, 1998.

Orwell, G., *The Collected Essays Journalism and Letters of George Orwell*, vol. 3, New York, Harcourt, Brace and World, 1968.

Pareto, V., *Manuel d'économie politique*, 2nd edn, Paris, M. Giard, 1927.

van Parijs, P., *Real Freedom for All: What (if anything) can Justify Capitalism?*, Oxford, Oxford University Press, 1995.

Pinker, S., *The Blank Slate: The Modern Denial of Human Nature*, London, Penguin, 2003.

Plant, R., 'Hayek on Social Justice: A Critique', in Birner, J. and van Zijp, R. (eds), *Hayek, Co-ordination and Evolution*, London: Routledge, 1994, pp. 175–176.

Popper, K., *The Poverty of Historicism*, London, Routledge, (1944/1945, 1957) 2002.

—, *The Open Society and Its Enemies*, vol. I, London, Routledge and Kegan Paul, 1945.

Quinton, A., 'Introduction', in Quinton, A. (ed.), *Political Philosophy*, Oxford, Oxford University Press, 1967.

Rawls, J., *A Theory of Justice*, Oxford, Oxford University Press, 1971.

—, *Political Liberalism*, New York, Columbia University Press, 1993.

Raz, J., 'The Rule of Law and Its Virtue', in Raz, J. (ed.), *The Authority of Law: Essays on Law and Morality*, Oxford, Oxford University Press, (1977) 1983, pp. 210–232.

Robbins, L., 'Hayek on Liberty', *Economica*, February 1961, pp. 66–81.

Rosenblatt, F., 'The Perceptron: A Probabilistic Model for Information Storage and Organization in the Brain', *Psychological Review*, vol. 65, 1958, pp. 386–408.

Russell, B., 'Analogy', in Russell, B. (ed.), *Human Knowledge: Its Scope and Limits*, Abingdon, Routledge (1948) 2009, pp. 425–428.

Rutherford, S., *Lex, Rex*, Ashburn, Hess Publishing, (1644) 1998.

Sandel, M., *Liberalism and the Limits of Justice*, Cambridge, Cambridge University Press, 1982.

Scruton, R., *The Meaning of Conservatism*, London, MacMillan, 1980.

—, 'In Defence of the Nation', in Scruton, R. (ed.), *The Philosopher on Dover Beach*, London, St. Martin's Press, 1990, pp. 299–328.

—, 'The First Person Plural', in Beiner, R. (ed.), *Theorizing Nationalism*, New York, SUNY Press, 1999, pp. 279–293.

—, 'Hayek and Conservatism', in Feser, E. (ed.), *The Cambridge Companion to Hayek*, Cambridge, Cambridge University Press, 2006, pp. 208–231.

Shklar, J., 'Political Theory and the Rule of Law', in Shklar, J. (ed.), *Political Thought and Political Thinkers*, Chicago, University of Chicago Press, (1987) 1998, pp. 37–21.

Skidelsky, R., 'Hayek versus Keynes: The Road to Reconciliation', in Feser, E. (ed.) *The Cambridge Companion to Hayek*, Cambridge, Cambridge University Press, 2006, pp. 82–110.

Steele, D. R., *From Marx to Mises: Post-Capitalist Society and the Challenge of Economic Calculation*, La Salle, Open Court, 1992.

Steele, G. R. *Keynes and Hayek: The Money Economy*, London, Routledge, 2001.

—, *The Economics of Friedrich Hayek*, Basingstoke, Palgrave MacMillan, 2nd edn, 2007.

Taylor, C., *Sources of the Self*, Harvard, Harvard University Press, 1989.

Tebble, A. J., 'Exclusion for Democracy', *Political Theory*, vol. 34, no. 4, 2006, pp. 463–487.

—, 'Hayek and Social Justice: A Critique', *Critical Review of International Social and Political Philosophy*, vol. 12, no. 4, 2009, pp. 581–604.

de Tocqueville, A., *Democracy in America*, London, Penguin Classics, (1835/1840) 2003.

Uebel, T. E., 'Some Scientism, Some Historicism, Some Critics', in Stone, M.W.F. and Wolff, J. (eds), *The Proper Ambition of Science*, London, Routledge, 2000, pp. 151–173.

Vanberg, V., 'Spontaneous Market Order and Social Rules: A Critical Examination of F. A. Hayek's Theory of Cultural Evolution', *Economics and Philosophy*, vol. 2, April 1986, pp. 75–100.

Vaughn, K., 'The Mengerian Roots of the Austrian Revival', in Caldwell, B. (ed.), *Carl Menger and his Legacy in Economics*, Durham, Duke University Press, 1990, pp. 379–407.

Viner, J., 'Hayek on Freedom and Coercion', *Southern Economic Journal*, vol. 27, January 1961, pp. 230–236.

Walras, L., *Elements of Pure Economics*, London, Routledge, (1874) 2003.

Walzer, M., *Spheres of Justice*, New York, Basic Books, 1983.

Watkins, J. W. N., '[Review of] Hayek, *The Counter-Revolution of Science*', *Ethics*, vol. 64, no. 1, 1953, pp. 56–59.

Wootton, B., *Freedom under Planning*, London, George Allen and Unwin, 1945.

Young, I. M., *Justice and the Politics of Difference*, Princeton, Princeton University Press, 1990.

Zamyatin, Y. *We*, New York, EOS Publishing, (1921) 1999.

Index